Thinking Skills Workbook

by Jonathan Hussey and Jo Richardson

BENNION KEARNY

Published in 2013 by Bennion Kearny Limited.

Copyright © Bennion Kearny Ltd 2013

ISBN: 978-1-909125-30-8

All Rights Reserved. No part of this publication may be reproduced, stored in a retrieval system, or transmitted in any form or by any means, electronic, mechanical, photocopying, recording or otherwise, without the prior permission of the publisher.

This book is sold subject to the condition that it shall not, by way of trade or otherwise, be lent, re-sold, hired out or otherwise circulated without the publisher's prior consent in any form of binding or cover other than that it which it is published and without a similar condition including this condition being imposed on the subsequent purchaser.

Bennion Kearny has endeavoured to provide trademark information about all the companies and products mentioned in this book by the appropriate use of capitals. However, Bennion Kearny cannot guarantee the accuracy of this information.

Published by Bennion Kearny Limited
6 Victory House
64 Trafalgar Road
Birmingham
B13 8BU

www.BennionKearny.com

Cover image: © AirOne

About the Authors

Jonathan Hussey is one of the most exciting innovators of interventions for rehabilitating offenders today. He holds a B.Sc. (Hons) in Psychology from Loughborough University and a B.A. (Hons) in Community Justice Studies from Portsmouth University, as well as being a fully qualified, experienced, and award winning Probation Officer. Jonathan has worked extensively in the Criminal Justice System, but has specialised in leading roles within the Probation Service and Youth Offending Services. Jonathan currently works as a consultant for the Probation Service, and has established a successful training company; Intervention Consultancy (www.reoffending.org.uk).

Jo Richardson joined the Probation Service in 2005, initially within the Employment, Training and Education team before working as a Probation Officer from 2006. She works within a generic team managing offenders who pose a medium or high risk of serious harm to the public, including those within medium and high security mental health facilities, and of an extensive age range from young adults to elderly offenders. She is also trained as an Aggression Replacement Training (ART) facilitator, delivering this to both male and female offenders. Both her roles within the Probation Service have involved a high level of multi-agency working, including increasing the awareness of other agencies to the role of the Probation Service. Jo holds a BA (Hons) Community Justice, Portsmouth.

Should you, or your organisation, require training on the delivery of these workbooks, then please contact Jonathan Hussey and Jo Richardson at interventioninfo@ymail.com

Table of Contents

Preface   **1**
The use of language   1
The purpose of this workbook   1
Who this workbook is for   2
What this workbook covers   4
Delivering the exercises   6

Section One   **8**
Cognitive Behavioural Therapy   8
Cycle of Change   8
The Ripple Effect   11
What are Cognitive Distortions?   11
What is Motivational Interviewing?   13
How to do Motivational Interviewing   14
What are Learning Styles   15
Strategies for Tackling Offending Behaviour   17
Bibliography   20

Section Two   **21**
The Exercises   21
Exercise 1 – The My Trigger Triangle   22
Exercise 2 – Problem Solving Sequence   31
Exercise 3 – Defining a Problem   42
Exercise 4 – Being Exact   53
Exercise 5 – Brain Storming Exercise   62
Exercise 6 – Perspective Taking   68
Exercise 7 - The Ripple Effect   76
Exercise 8 – Consequential Thinking   84
Exercise 9 - Decision scale: How do I pick?   94
Exercise 10 – Ending and Reviews (the 3R's)   105

Exercise 11 – Problem Solving Sequence Reviewed   116
Exercise 12 – Reflections   122

Preface

How do you address an individual who commits crimes with little, or no, awareness as to how their choices have led them offend? Do we just tell them what they did was wrong and that they should have behaved differently? Or do we help the perpetrators of crime come to an understanding themselves - to create that 'light bulb' moment related to consequential thinking and their own unique control over their lives? Surely, if we believe people can change, then the latter will facilitate a better sustained change in an offender's behaviour? Developing this form of consequential thinking, and helping bring about a general increase in thinking skills, is what this workbook sets out to achieve.

The use of language

In the following pages, this workbook will refer to the *facilitator, practitioner* or *tutor*. These terms mean the individual *delivering exercises* to the other person. These terms are interchanged, depending on the context, but they all mean the same thing here.

In turn, the following terms will refer to the person at whom the exercise is directed: *client*, *participant* and *offender*. Again these terms are interchanged, depending on the context.

The purpose of this workbook

The purpose of this workbook is to give the facilitator of any exercise an *easy-to-follow structure* to work from - with the client - to help build and increase consequential thinking skills and provide a structure for problem solving.

In order to do this, this workbook is specifically designed to help the client consider the sequence of events leading to their offending, the alternatives which may have been open to them, and how to review and revise their own behaviour. By doing so, the motivation to 'change', and arguably also the ability to change, should build up within the client. The exercises in this workbook, therefore, seek to help the client build a conscious recognition of the impact their behaviour has on both their own life, and the lives of those around them.

Of course, this workbook does not claim that by completing the exercises the client will definitely have an increased level of consequential thinking. However, if the facilitator can get the client to see and take responsibility for their behaviour, it will hopefully act as an additional barrier to future problematic or offending behaviour.

As with all cognitive behavioural work, the majority of the exercises here are designed to create ambivalence (see section one) within the offender regarding their view as to the impact of their problematic behaviour.

Who this workbook is for and the target client base

This workbook can be used on a one-to-one basis or adapted for use with a small group. It should primarily be used by individuals who work with offenders, including professionals in the Probation and Prison Service; this is why much of the emphasis is placed on offending behaviour. However, other professionals within schools and drug or alcohol agencies may also benefit from the information contained in this workbook.

The targeted clients should have, at the very least, a basic level of literacy and prove motivated to discuss their problematic behaviour. Those who fully deny their offences or problematic behaviour, who say, for example "I have no problems and do not want to talk about it!" should not be considered suitable for the exercises in this workbook. Should the client, at the very least, accept that something *did happen* or prove willing to talk about 'some' of their behaviour then they can be considered suitable.

It is worth recognising here, that many offenders may deny all, or parts, of their behaviour. This is perfectly normal as many clients may use denial as a means of justifying, accepting, or coping with negative behaviour. Should you wish to learn more about addressing denial then look out for our separate workbook on this topic.

When considering working with offenders specifically, the exercises within this workbook are applicable to most offenders and offence types. However, there are examples where the facilitator will need to modify, edit, or simply leave out an exercise. Care must also be given to challenge 'inappropriate' answers, with enough time planned for each session to cover this. Inappropriate answers in this instance could be something which indicates the offender is thinking in a rigid manner, for example stating that "There were no other choices open to me", or anything which indicates that the offender feels there was no 'time' before the offence to change their course of action. This might take the form of "I didn't plan it" or "It just happened" to stating that they were under someone/something else's control.

Always be prepared to challenge inappropriate answers as they arise and in a motivational style (see section one). So, with this in mind, compare the brief conversations below and consider how this plays out in a session:

Practitioner: Tell me about the moments before you chose to commit the offence.

Offender: There weren't any 'moments', I've told you before, it all just happened in a big blur.

Practitioner: Well, that's an inappropriate comment. Of course there was time before the offence. Do you just not understand the question?

Offender: Are you calling me thick or something? You weren't there. You don't know what happened.

Practitioner: I know what was likely to have happened and I've got the CPS papers. You are trying to deny responsibility for your offending but only you are in control of your actions.

Offender: Seriously, are you listening to me? Are you just plain thick or what? [walks out]

Compared to…

Practitioner: Tell me about the moments before you chose to commit the offence.

Offender: There weren't any 'moments', I've told you before, it all just happened in a big blur.

Practitioner: Okay, go back to the last clear memory you have before the blur and describe that to me.

Offender: I was out with friends, and we'd missed the last bus home. The next thing I know, we're all piling into a car and then there's blue lights behind us.

Practitioner: Tell me about 'piling in to the car'; where did the car come from? Who was driving?

Offender: I was driving, you know that. One of my mates dared me to.

Practitioner: How else could you have responded to that dare?

Offender: I don't know. I always take people up on a dare, it's my thing.

Practitioner: Well, let's look now at what else you could have done at that point in time, just before the offence.

Offender: This isn't going to be real for me. You'll just say things like I should have said no.

Practitioner: Well, if you do it with me then you can make sure the options we come up with are real.

Offender: This should be interesting – fine, come on then.

What this workbook covers

This workbook is divided into two main sections.

Section One

This section covers some of the basic theoretical knowledge needed by the facilitator to undertake the accompanying exercises. It covers: What is Cognitive Behavioural Therapy (CBT), The Cycle of Change, Motivational Interviewing, The Ripple Effect, 'Thinking Errors', and learning styles. Following an exploration into what each element is, we will explain briefly, where possible, how to undertake the relevant skill.

Note: Should the facilitator already know these skills, then they can simply begin the exercises.

Caution: Section one is primarily for the practitioner's reference and is not designed to be shared with the offender. In our experience, it is useful for the practitioner to have some background knowledge of the history of working with offending behaviour - particularly if an offender needs to be challenged as to the 'point' of the work being undertaken. As such, there may be times when it is appropriate to discuss elements contained within section one.

Section Two

Section two covers the workbook exercises themselves. Here we shall explain exercises that will help the client increase their consequential thinking.

Exercises within the workbook are designed to be completed as a course, with the end aim of having learned the 'problem solving sequence'. Exercises are broadly grouped into either *general thinking skills, defining problems, generating options, or weighing up problems.*

Note: Where appropriate, the facilitator can use the exercises as standalone tasks depending on the assessed needs of the client; however it is recommended that the exercises are run sequentially.

When assessing the client's needs, the facilitator must use their professional judgement as to where the client resides in the cycle of change (see section one) *and then* decide which exercises are relevant.

Should the facilitator want to run the exercises as a form of 'programme', then we suggest the following sequence:

1. **The Cognitive Behavioural Triangle**: This helps the client understand the link between thinking, feeling and behaviour. *General thinking skills*

2. **The Problem Solving Sequence**: Gives the client a structure to work from when confronted with difficult problems. *General thinking skills*

3. **Defining a Problem**: Provides the client with a methodology to identify what the actual problem is. *Defining a problem*

4. **Being Exact**: Provides more on defining problems. This exercise helps the offender to boil the problem down to its constituent, and importantly, achievable parts. *Defining problems*

5. **Brainstorming Exercise**: Here the tutor will be seeking to help the offender understand how to generate options to solve their problems. *Generating options*

6. **Perspective Taking**: This exercise looks at 'perspectives' with the client. The purpose being to stress to the client the importance of the concept that everyone can see things in a different way. *General thinking skills*

7. **The Ripple Effect**: In this exercise the tutor will explore what is known as the ripple effect. *Weighing up options*

8. **Consequential Thinking**: Helps the client consider how to respond to a problem. *Weighing up options*

9. **Decision Scale**: This exercise helps the client consider more on how to respond to problems. *Weighing up options*

10. **The 3 R's**: This exercise looks at how to manage the outcomes of problem solving. *Weighing up options*

11. **The Problem Solving Sequence Reviewed**: Helps the facilitator review with the client the problem solving sequence and learning points. *General thinking skills*

12. **Reflections**: Helping the client begin the process of being introspective about themselves. *General thinking skills*

Delivering the Exercises

Prior to each exercise, the facilitator will see **Tutor Notes**. These will give either step-by-step or descriptive guidance on how to run each exercise. The facilitator should read the notes and follow them. The subsequent worksheets(s) for the client follows the Tutor Notes.

Regardless of whether the exercises are being delivered as a single session, or as a sequential programme, they should always be completed with a simple verbal 'summing-up' of what was covered at the end of each exercise.

Tip: the facilitator should never start a session without thinking carefully about, and planning for, examples of answers that the offender may offer. It may sound obvious but if the facilitator is stumped by a question then the exercise can lose its intended impact. This also helps prepare the facilitator to address potentially inappropriate or anti-social answers.

Lastly, when undertaking any exercise, the facilitator should never be afraid to use a *neutral* example from their own lives as an illustration of the types of answers that the exercise is attempting to draw out from the client. However, these examples should **not** be deeply personal – these exercises are for the client, not therapy for the facilitator, nor to place the facilitator at risk.

Out of Session Work (optional)

Following each exercise, and to offer more to the client - thus reinforcing learning - optional out of session work is also suggested. These out of session work exercises can be used if the practitioner feels that it would be beneficial for the offender. However, it is not a required part of proceedings.

Adapting the Sessions and Alternative Exercises

Understanding a client's *learning style* (see section one) is imperative for ensuring that the client really understands what is being put to them by the tutor. Therefore, within this workbook, we also offer an alternative way to deliver each exercise where possible.

Section One

Cognitive Behavioural Therapy

This workbook uses the theoretical basis of Cognitive Behavioural Therapy (CBT). Cognitive behaviourism as a whole, and in relation to working with offenders, works towards achieving a sense of personal responsibility within the offender for their behaviour and the resultant consequences (Chui, 2003:68-9). So, if the facilitator can motivate the offender to take responsibility for their behaviour and consider the consequences of their negative actions, then the offender may change their negative behaviours accordingly. But how does CBT enable the facilitator to do this?

CBT in itself is a form of therapy which aims to create an 'ability' in the person to address their problems. Unlike other therapies, it is rooted in the 'now' and looks at how our emotions colour how we approach any given situation. It also helps the client to understand how previous experiences may have shaped our current values and behaviour.

Through CBT, an offender can come to understand their own motives better, and challenge their problematic behaviour; replacing it with more pro social actions. In basic terms, the CBT approach believes that by changing someone's thinking, especially 'flawed' thinking, the resultant behaviour will also change. So, in keeping with the CBT approach, within this workbook, the exercises we propose will help the client consider the implications of their actions by changing their thinking.

The Cycle of Change

The *Cycle of Change* was developed by DiClemente and Prochaska as an aid to assist people in understanding why some people are able to make (and sustain changes) whilst others fail to recognise the need for change. It is also a model that provides a foundation for understanding the stages an individual 'progresses through' when trying to change their behaviour.

The Cycle of Change very simply breaks down the process of change into six areas defined by a person's motivation, and indeed ability, to change (Hussey 2012). We believe that it is critical that the facilitator understands the concept of the Cycle Of Change because one of the aims of this workbook is to increase the client's internal level of motivation to change by, at the very least, moving them firmly into the *contemplation phase* of this cycle, if not through to the *preparation phase*. So, what are these phases?

Using an offender as an example again, initially, a person may begin in a stage called *pre contemplation*, where there is no recognition of an existing problem. With offenders, this can be seen as a state of denial related to either the offence or the harm it has caused.

Through creating ambivalence towards an offender's current lifestyle, movement can be made towards *contemplation* where a person begins to identify drawbacks to their choices and starts to desire change.

The next stages are *Preparation* (also known as *decision*) and *action*. *Preparation* to change and *action* are rather self-explanatory. These phases often occur in quick succession as the motivation brought about by a decision to change behaviour feeds into the actions to alter their behaviour in accordance with their newly desired decision(s). If progress through these stages is achieved, then the person can move forwards to *maintenance* (Fleet and Annison, 2003; Winstone and Hobbs, 2006:262-8).

Note: Should the client conclude in the decision phase that change is too difficult, or 'not worth the effort', this results in a return to a state of pre contemplation.

Assuming that the client is now in a stage of maintenance, there is some debate about the next movement of the client. This debate centres around whether, having made a change, a person remains in the maintenance phase permanently, or whether he/she leaves the cycle when that change becomes internalised or a 'habit'.

As stated in Hussey (2012), for some to remain in the cycle forever is a rather depressing thought and so to aim to practice and perfect a change, to the point where exiting the cycle in a positive manner is achievable, can be a more encouraging viewpoint.

As mentioned above, the potential to exit the cycle at any stage through a lapse or relapse to old behaviours is always possible. A 'lapse' tends to refer to a momentary slip to previous behaviours, which can subsequently lead to either a return to the cycle or an exit from the cycle via a 'relapse' and the abandonment of change (Winstone and Hobbs, 2006:262-8).

For the visual learners amongst you, here is a diagram of the Cycle of Change:

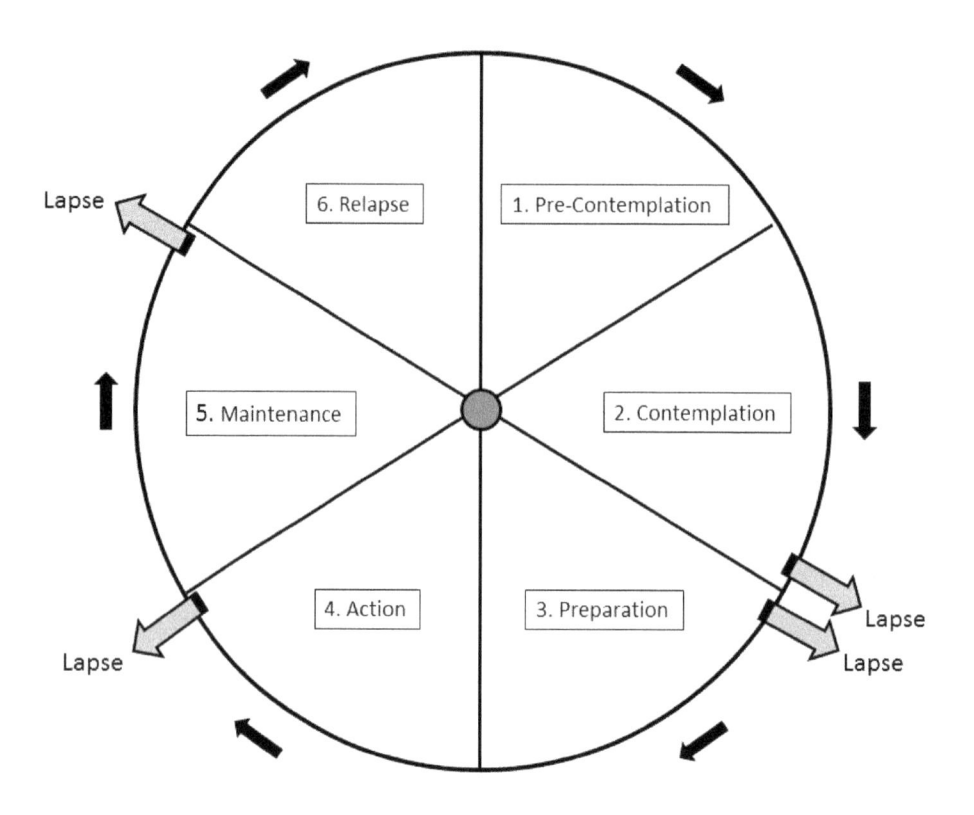

```
        6. Relapse      1. Pre-Contemplation
Lapse

        5. Maintenance   2. Contemplation

        4. Action        3. Preparation    Lapse
Lapse                                      Lapse
```

How to use the Cycle of Change

Using an offender who has just been sentenced as an example, and anticipating that the offender who undertakes the exercises is at the beginning of their sentence, we will assume that they are in the pre contemplation stage (with a belief that they do not need to change) regarding their offending behaviour. Here, the practitioner would use their understanding of the Cycle of Change to create ambivalence within the offender concerning offending - in an attempt to move them to the next stage of contemplation. To do this, the practitioner should try to create doubt in the client about the validity and worthwhileness of the offending behaviour. The facilitator should also try to encourage the offender to (at least) entertain the idea that there are other options. This stage can very much be the 'drip drip' approach to eroding seemingly set ideas.

Once an offender has moved into the contemplation stage, where they are open to discussing and even admitting that their offending behaviour is harmful, more work can be undertaken to underpin this theoretical shift; in particular the way the offender views the world towards more concrete behavioural choices and actions. This period can be a very unnerving time for the offender because they are, in many ways, 'undoing' what they thought they knew. So if this happens, and they start to move back to pre contemplation, the facilitator should do their best to support the offender in considering new options and moving them to the decision stage where there is a conscious choice to change.

Note: See how the above says 'assist' and 'support' not *advise*. Advice is a very thorny topic; no one generally wants to be told what to do and even when it is given, accepted and acted upon, then it will probably not be a lasting change as it *was not that person's choice*. The practitioner is there to help the offender make new decisions, not tell them what they should be doing (no matter how tempting this may be) under the guise of 'advice'.

Once the offender has decided to change and puts their new thoughts into action, it is here that the facilitator should discuss with them the obstacles of maintaining their new path. The reason for this is not to be negative or to encourage them to fail, but to allow them to realise and accept how it is going to be a difficult transition and that they should not just give up at the first hurdle, or indeed lapse.

The 'Ripple Effect'

The idea of the 'ripple effect' is the notion that whatever actions we do and whatever decisions we make, no matter how big or small, there are consequences and repercussions beyond what we may have expected for the original behaviour. There are several ways of visualising this; there is the classic 'butterfly flapping its wings in the amazon causing a typhoon in Japan', or more subtly, the rings of water reaching out to a pond's edge following a stone being dropped into the water. Another example might even be the tectonic movement of the Earth's plates – they move at the pace of fingernail growth but they still cause the formation of mountains. When discussing this idea with an offender, it needs to be applied so that they begin to understand that whilst they may consider their offence 'minor', the unintentional impacts above those directly involved can be immense. The aim is to remove a client's blinkers and increase self-awareness with regard to the community and society.

What are Cognitive Distortions ('thinking errors') and how can they be recognised?

In order to move offenders forward within the Cycle of Change, this workbook seeks to explore the impact and consequences of the client's behaviour (with the client) on themselves, and the community, and in doing so raise their awareness of the impact of their choices.

Here, caution should always be exercised in order to prevent the client from building up cognitive distortions. But what are cognitive distortions?

In brief, a cognitive distortion is a 'thinking error' (Hussey 2012). It is a particular way of looking at a fact, or part of life, which acts to overemphasise or exaggerate that issue, often leaving no alternative or way back once identified as 'fact'. For example, an offender may have decided that 'all the Police' hate them and therefore be unable to consider approaching authority for assistance. The fact that very few people are 'always' targeted by Police, and that all Police Officers will differ in their approach towards their treatment of offenders, and that each meeting with the Police is likely to be a different experience is too much detail for the distortion and as such these facts are dismissed by the offender's thinking error.

Sometimes, a cognitive distortion can be a comfortable way of thinking for an offender (or anyone for that matter) even if it is incredibly negative and damaging, because there are no subtleties or unknowns. Therefore change is difficult.

Cognitive distortions do not always lead to offending behaviour and examples of distortions can be found in most aspects of life. However, where distortions related to offending are identified, they can be key in understanding both why an offender chooses to behave in such a manner, and also how to address that behaviour. Using the 'trigger triangle', covered later, cognitive distortions provide an illustration of the possible thoughts which are feeding an individual's offending behaviour.

Cognitive distortions are typically associated with depressive thinking and there are many different types of cognitive distortions. Discussion of these is beyond this workbook. Knowledge of them can be gained from further reading and practitioners may find such additional reading useful. Should you want to read more on the types of thinking errors then a useful book in exploring these is the related book (written by this one of this workbook's co-authors, Jonathan Hussey) entitled: *Reoffending: a practitioner's guide to addressing offending behaviour in the Criminal Justice System*.

A working example of a cognitive distortion from real life practice could be when an offender tells themselves: "I am a bad person" when, in fact, it is only part of their behaviour which is bad. They may, in fact, be a very pleasant person ninety-nine percent of the time and it is only one percent of the time when their behaviour can be seen as 'bad' or antisocial. This type of thinking error or cognitive distortion is called over-generalising. So, by highlighting the cognitive distortion to the offender, and breaking it down through exercises, the offender is given the opportunity to adjust their thinking and change their behaviour.

When considering the above, it is the internal dialogue which will enable an offender to move through the Cycle of Change and it is therefore envisaged that the practitioner will support thinking skills work with other offending behaviour work, as well as more holistic support, running concurrently.

What is Motivational Interviewing?

Motivational Interviewing (MI) is a method of working with offenders created by Miller and Rollnick (1991). Where other methods may build a relationship in which change can happen - MI provides a method of progressing and directing that change.

MI is a particular way of facilitating the recognition of problems and addressing them; motivation is a fluctuating state and MI uses a systematic strategy to build internal motivation to tackle these - rather than external pressure (Miller and Rollnick, 1991 cited in Fleet and Annison, 2003:133), linking it to normative compliance. Confrontation is an aim of, rather than a process of, MI (Winstone and Hobbs, 2006:259). However, it is important to note that this confrontation is not code for 'argument' with the offender. The confrontation regards their ideas and statements.

There are five key principles:

1. Being empathetic and accepting of the individual although not the behaviour
2. The development of discrepancies in an offender's cognitive distortions leading to the questioning of beliefs
3. The avoidance of argument through rolling with resistance
4. Seeing resistance as part of an offender's reaction to discomfort with the realisation of their cognitive distortions
5. Supporting efficacy through building belief in the offender's own abilities

(Fleet and Annison, 2003:133-6).

MI is often linked to the Cycle of Change as its principles can be integrated into the cycle. A substantial advantage to MI is that it can be delivered effectively in one session. MI also introduces protective factors which can be considered as reasons to sustain any changes made within a lifestyle. Ideally these protective factors would be internal beliefs rather than external, as the potential for an external factor to change or 'let down' the offender (if it were a person they were changing 'for', for example) can create the potential for lapse (Winstone and Hobbs, 2006:284). It is worth noting, however, that female offenders may pick an external factor such as their child and that this could be linked to social bond theory considerations such that family responsibilities are likely to cause desistance in female offenders (Rex, 1999:374).

As with any approach, there are no guarantees for success; an offender may exit the Cycle of Change by decision if they determine that they are content with their current lifestyle and the process of using MI would need to begin again.

How to do Motivational Interviewing

MI involves being able to direct a conversation with a person so that they are able to discover a truth for themselves. The practitioner needs to be able to read the feedback from the person sat with them in the form of both verbal and non-verbal communication. Listening to what the person is trying to say and reflecting this back to them, either to highlight a discrepancy with their statements or to enable them to find the meaning, are crucial skills. Unhelpful statements are those that contain advice, threats, criticism or direct commands - however tempting.

During any one session, several things are important; being specific in the feedback that is given to the offender (especially praise), listening carefully to the client, using both summarising and reflective listening to prove that the client has been heard, making sure questions are open questions, and encouraging self-motivating questions. These are all evidence that MI is in use.

If the offender resists or is disruptive then change the practice approach, do not attempt to force them to change.

An example discussion using MI:

Practitioner: Thank you for being punctual. I've noticed that you've been on time the last two sessions. Today we need to look again at your index offence.

Offender: Again? I've told you, it just happened, I don't plan these things.

Practitioner: So you're telling me that you think you had no choice in whether you committed the offence or not?

Offender: That's not what I said, you're twisting my words.

Practitioner: Explain to me what you meant?

Offender: It's just when I'm out with certain people, things just happen. You know, take on a life of their own.

Practitioner: So you feel it's your friends' fault for making you act in a particular way and leading you astray.

Offender: Not their fault exactly, but they always let me go too far.

Practitioner: They 'let you'? As in they give you permission?

Offender: What? No! They just don't stop me. It's not like I have any other choices. Look can we leave this, you're just twisting what I mean.

Practitioner: No worries. Let's look at your plans for this weekend instead

Offender: I'm out with my friends, we're going to that new club out of town.

Practitioner: Tell me how you picture that night going, and ending.

Offender: I don't. It'll just be fun. Lots of drinks and laughs.

Practitioner: And that's what happened last time you went out with the same friends?

Offender: Yeah, sort of. Well, no – at the end I got nicked. I told you, it always gets carried away.

Practitioner: You did tell me that these friends let you 'go too far' but that you had no other options at the time. Are these your hopes for the weekend too?

Offender: No, not really.

Practitioner: In which case, let's use today's session to look at what options might be available to you so that the weekend is a fun one.

Offender: Fine, if we must.

What are Learning Styles? What are the factors to consider for each style?

We do not all learn in the same manner, and learning styles are a way of recognising this. There are three main recognised ways in which we learn:

Auditory: where preference is given to listening to relayed information through lectures or discussions.

Visual: where a person is best able to take in information they can 'see' in the form of presentations, books and diagrams.

Kinaesthetic: where learners prefer to 'do' in order to learn for themselves.

Evidence has shown that offenders tend to be kinaesthetic learners, requiring a participatory approach rather than a didactic one (Hopkinson and Rex, 2003:165) and this is worth bearing in mind when considering the manner in which to deliver an exercise, or whether it needs to be broken down over several sessions. There are various questionnaires available which can be completed with an offender to determine the best style of learning for them. However, caution should be exercised when labelling an offender as having a particular style. It is only a guide and not a necessity to subsequently present all information rigidly in that manner.

This workbook provides some examples of presenting the same exercise in different styles, however almost any exercise can be adapted. It doesn't have to be a complex process to change information from a diagram to spoken or as an 'experiment'. Below are three ways of presenting the same information regarding an offender's sentence:

Auditory Simply stating: "You were sentenced to three years in custody. You've now served half of that in prison and so been released. You will spend the rest of your sentence on licence. Part of that licence is to report weekly to Probation for supervision where we will undertake work to address issues related to your offending. If you fail to attend these appointments, or break any other conditions of release, such as committing another offence, then you may be recalled to prison."

Visual

[Diagram showing a timeline with boxes labelled: Sentence, Mid-point, Breach → Prison, End of Sentence above the line; Prison, Release, Probation below the line]

Kinaesthetic Chop the above diagram into pieces and ask the offender to reassemble the diagram (like a jigsaw) with discussion as to why they think pieces go in certain places.

Strategies for Tackling Offending Behaviour (optional reading)

Offenders are a heterogeneous group and any interventions for offending behaviour need to be able to recognise and manage this. Therefore the 'best' intervention in any given case is the one that fits with the needs and motivation of the offender; the motivation of the offender is the key point. Change cannot be forced but must be a conscious choice of the person.

The ability to change lifestyle patterns to avoid previous associations is an important factor in order to successfully sustain desistance (Rex, 1999:375). An offending lifestyle is a learned behaviour (Bandura, 1973 cited in Winstone and Hobbs, 2006:49), whether through family, friends or the general environment. This learned behaviour is then reinforced by socialisation experiences which promote, or accept, offending as appropriate. Things are compounded by information processing biases, whereby external events are internally filtered to reinforce the schema of the 'need' to offend in certain situations. Offending can also be related to different underpinning factors which are not in themselves viewed as criminogenic, such as low self-esteem. This then effects how, or whether, any intervention (depending on its theoretical basis) can be effective (Cameron and Telfer, 2004:49).

JoHari's window (Winstone and Hobbs, 2006:239) is a useful tool for both understanding offending and enabling an offender to understand their own offending. JoHari's window, so called as is it named after its creators, is a way of sorting and compartmentalising information about ourselves. A grid, as below, is used and key facts can be sorted accordingly. Some of the grid requires feedback from those around the person.

	Known to self	Not Known to self
Known to Others	Public	Blind spot
Not Known to Others	Private	Uncharted

Information which is known to both the client and to others can be considered in the public domain. That which is known only to the client is private. It needs to be understood by a practitioner that asking a client to share information can mean the client moving that information from a private domain to a public one; this in itself can prove an inherent difficulty for some people.

Facts which are seen by others but not recognised by the person concerned exists in their 'blind spot'; for someone who is pre contemplative it may well be that much information lies in this category. The final square is information which is totally unknown, uncharted waters for all. This square can be seen as containing someone's potential.

A point made by the Cognitive Centre Foundation (1999 cited in Winstone and Hobbs 2006:284) concerns the need for feedback to increase 'awareness about self' leading to the potential for self management, in line with the ideas of JoHari's window as described. In other words, bringing information into the public domain. This feedback should take the form of generating alternative options and consequences, which leaves the choice of action to the offender and so does not challenge their autonomy. It is not moralising as it remains sensitive to diversity and disapproves of the anti-social behaviour of a person, not the person themselves. Any person working with an offender is ideally placed to facilitate this feedback.

A further but vitally important consideration is the wider social environment of the offender and the impact this may have on their ability to desist (Chui, 2003:69). Many interventions are not able to change the social environment or meet welfare needs, as they concentrate on criminogenic needs as per the cognitive behavioural approach. Whilst this provides much needed social skills, or social capital, in many cases, it cannot provide the human capital to continue desistance when any immediate threat sanctions for continued anti-social behaviour or offending are lifted. It could be argued that welfare needs are not the concern of any organisation whose role is to address offending and this can be addressed through other means. However, such a narrow scope for an intervention can lead to offenders being 'factory processed' (Hopkinson and Rex, 2003:170), which would rather undermine the values of rehabilitation.

A practitioner working with an offender is likely to come under the label of 'authority', at least to the offender themselves. Thoughts on the use of authority could be associated with the current popularity of 'treatment' of offending behaviour, which refers back to a medical model of working with offenders where they were considered to be 'deficient' and requiring 'curing'. This approach can create an image of 'the other', with offenders being viewed as different to the population in general and so can be exclusionary (Mair, 2004 cited in Davies, Croall and Tyrer, 2005:411). Interventions which use cognitive behavioural methods are able to 'treat deficits' in thinking skills in an inclusive manner through encouraging social ties and therefore social capital (McNeill, 2003:155).
Another thought on the use of authority is that of legitimacy and normative compliance. If offenders view the use of authority by the professional as legitimate rather than threatening or coercive, there is a greater chance that compliance will be normative. Normative compliance refers to abiding by law or rules through agreement with the

structure in which they are placed and a belief of obligation towards obeisance; rather than compliance due to constraint methods, or through self-interest, or even because of habit (Faulkner, 2002 cited in Winstone and Hobbs, 2006:293).

Finally, it must also be remembered that there is typically a 'zigzag' pattern of desistance, as offending or not is not a binary concept (Burnett, 2000 cited in McNeill, 2003:151). The risk of harm may well reduce before complete desistance is reached (Friendship, Beech and Browne, 2002:442-2).

Bibliography

Cameron, H. and Telfer, J. (2004) Cognitive-Behavioural Group Work and Its Application to Specific Offender Groups. *The Howard Journal*, 43(1), pp.47-64

Chui, W. H. (2003) What Works in Reducing Re-Offending: Principles and Programmes. In W. H. Chui and M. Nellis (Eds.) *Moving Probation Forwards: Evidence, Arguments and Practice*. pp56-70, Pearson Longman: Essex

Davies, M. Croall, H. and Tyrer, J. (2005) *Criminal Justice. An Introduction to the Criminal Justice System in England and Wales*. Pearson Longman: Harlow

Fleet, F. and Annison, J. (2003) In Support of Effectiveness: Facilitating Participation and Sustaining Change. In W. H. Chui and M. Nellis (Eds.) *Moving Probation Forwards: Evidence, Arguments and Practice*. pp129-143, Pearson Longman: Essex

Friendship, C., Beech, A. R. and Browne, K. D. (2002) Reconviction As An Outcome Measure In Research. *The British Journal of Criminology*, 42, 442-444

Hopkinson, J. and Rex, S. (2003) Essential Skills In Working With Offenders. In W. H. Chui and M. Nellis (Eds.) *Moving Probation Forwards: Evidence, Arguments and Practice*. pp.163-178 Pearson Longman: Essex

Hussey, J. (2012) *Reoffending: A practitioners Guide to Working With Offenders and Offending Behaviour in the Criminal Justice System*. Bennion Kearny: Birmingham

McNeill, F. (2003) Desistance-Focused Probation Practice. In W. H. Chui and M. Nellis (Eds.) *Moving Probation Forwards: Evidence, Arguments and Practice*. pp.146-191 Pearson Longman: Essex

McNeill, F. (2004) Desistance, Rehabilitation and Correctionalism: Developments and Prospects in Scotland. *The Howard Journal*, 43(4), 420-436

Rex, S. (1999) Desistance from Offending: Experiences of Probation, *The Howard Journal*, 38(4), 366-383

Winstone, J. and Hobbs, S. (2006) *Strategies for Tackling Offending Behaviour, Volume 2*. 231-395, University of Portsmouth: Portsmouth

Section 2

The Exercises

You can adapt the exercises to all variations of problematic behaviour, including those that do not necessarily include offending behaviour.

Despite our use of the term "offender", as discussed in section one of this workbook, this by no means excludes other problematic behaviours by the client which they freely admit too (i.e. behaviours not linked to a particular offence). This workbook is not only for adults but also ideal as a form of intervention for others, such as a young person who has maliciously pushed another pupil at college (where police action has not been deemed necessary) or indeed instances of bullying.

The exercises have been written for a target audience of both male and female clients, aged fifteen and older. However, should the facilitator feel that a younger person would benefit from this workbook, care would need to be taken to ensure the language and examples used within exercises are appropriate.

At the end of any exercise, the facilitator should ask the client what they have learned from that exercise. The answer should then be written onto the worksheet in the space provided at the end. The reason for this, is that once the facilitator has completed all the exercises they want to use with the client, the learning points (which are personal to the client) can be summarised and fed back to the client, in keeping with the MI style of working (see section one) and to demonstrate outcomes in turn.

Exercise 1 – The My Trigger Triangle

Category of exercise: General thinking skills

> **Tutor Notes**
>
> The Cognitive Behavioural Therapy (CBT) Triangle is an important element which, for the purposes of this workbook, should be explored first by the tutor with the offender. So, to undertake this exercise, the tutor will need to know what the CBT Triangle is within the context of this workbook.
>
> Here, the CBT Triangle demonstrates and emphasises the link that all behaviour is preceded by a thought and feeling. It is also represented in the diagrammatic form of a triangle (see worksheet).
>
> *Why is it important?* The tutor's aim is to get the client to become consciously aware, and in control, of the thoughts and feelings they have *before* any given action. The idea being that if a client can control their thoughts and feelings, then they can change their behaviour. So, for example, if the client develops more informed thoughts about a problem they are facing, it is hoped that they will then behave in a manner which is more conducive to solving problems.
>
> In this workbook, the CBT Triangle is re-named as *My Trigger Triangle*. The purpose of this is to give it a more personal feel to the offender. It is hoped that once the offender understands this exercise they can begin to 'own' their behaviour (take responsibility) as they become more consciously aware of their thoughts and feelings.

Step 1: Explain to the client that: "This triangle forms the basis of the work that you will be doing". Here it is a good idea for the tutor to explain a little about why it is important. You can use the explanation in the tutor notes should you wish.

Step 2: Show the client the Trigger Triangle diagram.

Step 3: Explain to the client that:

- Behaviour can always be controlled and is heavily affected by our thoughts and feelings.
- If we can change any element of this triangle, then we can change all the other parts too.

Step 4: Explain that before we explore this further, we will first look to *define* what thoughts, feelings and behaviour are.

Tip: Do not look to over-complicate this definition exercise but ensure that there is clarity on (at least) a very basic level of understanding. For example, simply seek to clarify the definitions as follows:

Thoughts: The things we think about in our mind; e.g. "I give up."

Feelings: The things we feel inside; e.g. "sad, happy, angry."

Behaviour: An action, the physical part of the triangle that can be seen by others; e.g. "ignoring someone."

Tip: It is important that the client understands the difference between thoughts and feelings. For example, "I am feeling sad" is a thought about a feeling, not a feeling in itself.

Step 5: Show the client the *'My Trigger Triangle'* diagram once again and ask the client to write under the headings, using their offence as the example of behaviour, what thoughts and feelings they had before it happened.

Tip: If the offender is particularly resistant to exploring their offence in this manner, at this time, then 'roll with the resistance' and allow them to pick another example to use. However, do make sure that the offence is revisited before the completion of the 'treatment' and a trigger triangle completed for it.

Step 6: Conclude the exercise by explaining what was originally set out in the exercise. This being: *all behaviour is preceded by a thought and feeling and if we can change our thoughts and feelings then we can change our actions.*

Tip: Here you may have to check that the client understands by asking them to give a further example to summarise what has been explored.

Exercise 1 – Worksheet

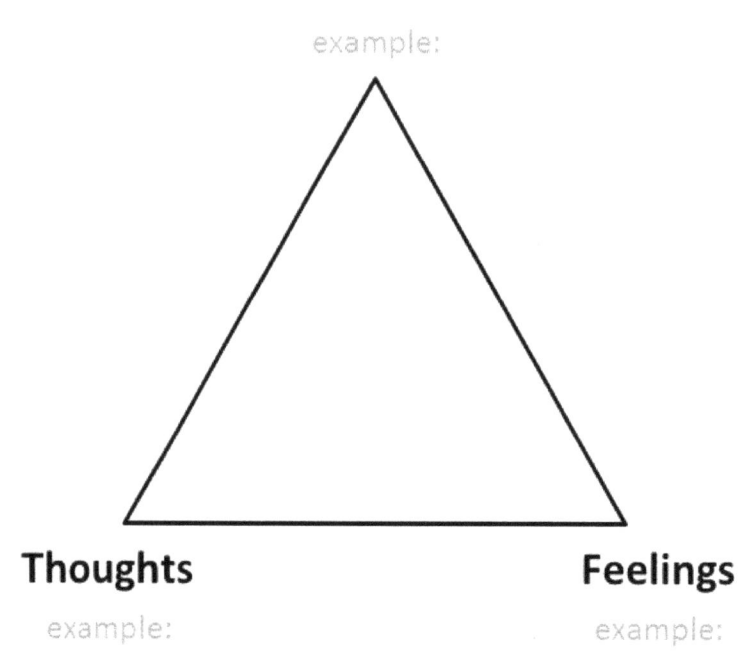

Behaviour
example:

Thoughts
example:

Feelings
example:

What is a Thought? Give an example:

What is a Feeling? Give an example:

What is Behaviour? Give an example:

Exercise 1a – Alternative Exercise

Step 1: Prepare nine flashcards with a picture depicting either a feeling, emotion or behaviour; three of each of these.

Step 2: Ask the offender to sort them in to three piles of 'feelings', 'thoughts' and 'behaviour'. Discuss their choices and provide guidance where appropriate.

Step 3: Ask the offender to arrange the cards on the trigger triangle at the appropriate point, depending on whether the card is depicting a thought, feeling or behaviour, so that a sequence is created relating to one particular event.

Step 4: To check understanding, ask the offender to draw three pictures on the blank cards to create their own set of 'feeling, behaviour and thought' cards based on a behaviour they do regularly. An easy one would be 'eating' – a feeling of hunger, a thought of wanting a takeaway, and a behaviour of ordering one.

Exercise 1a – Worksheet

(angry)	(happy)	(love)
I want to ignore it	It's Friday!	Let's get married!
Feeling	Thought	Behaviour

Exercise 1 – Out of Session Work

Should the tutor feel that more work on this is needed then they can present some optional work to be completed by the client outside of the session.

Step 1: Ask the client to complete a '*My Trigger Triangle*' for as many different situations as appropriate.

Step 2: Provide blank copies of the triangle and ask the offender to list - below the headings of thoughts, feelings, and behaviour - relevant examples for a specific situation that they have encountered in the week between sessions.

Tip: Generally, when this is completed, the wider the range of situations, the better the understanding of the triangle.

Exercise 1 – Out of Session Worksheet

Give an example of when a thought and feeling made you act in a specific way

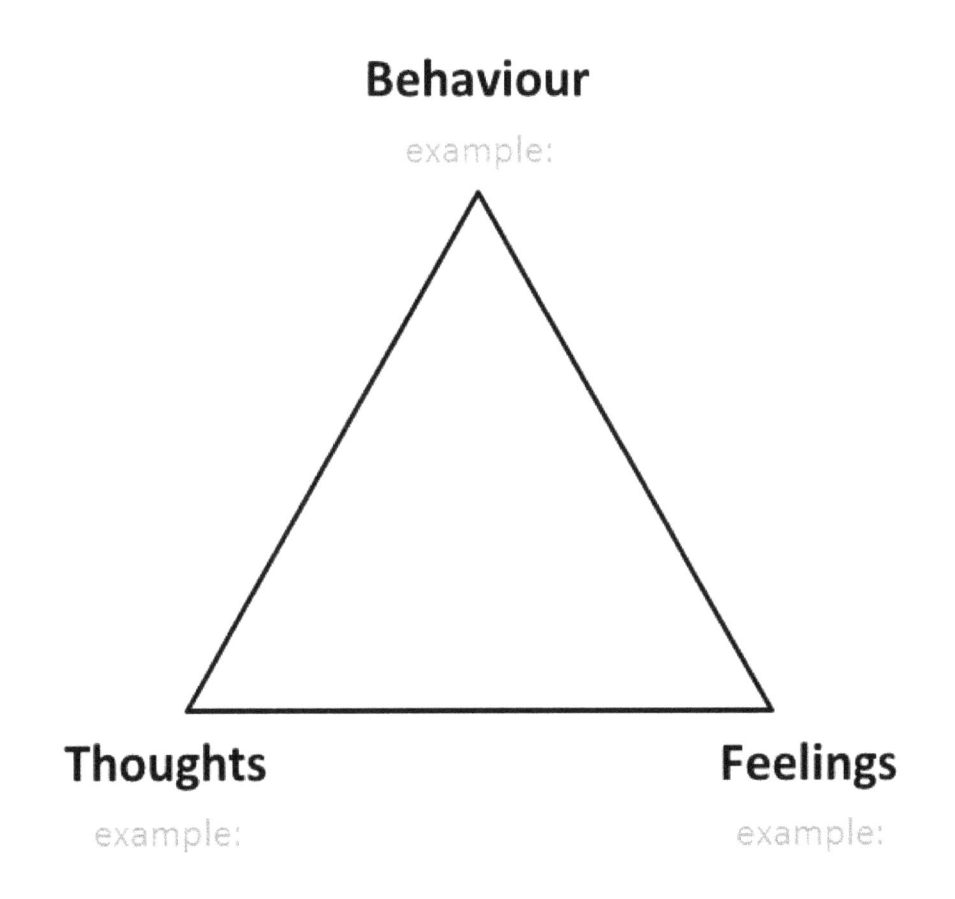

Behaviour

example:

Thoughts   **Feelings**

example: example:

Exercise 1 – Review

Name at least one thing that has been learned from this exercise.

Additional Notes:

Exercise 2 – Problem Solving Sequence

Category of exercise: General thinking skills

Tutor Notes

In order to be able to solve any given problem satisfactorily, there are several stages which need to be worked through. The following sequence is our suggestion of those stages in a memorable and understandable format. By breaking the process down into a sequence, with steps that can be learned, it is hoped that the overarching process of 'problem solving' becomes less of a mountain and more of a molehill.

It would be helpful, if the practitioner is intending to complete the workbook as a course, to keep a copy of the sequence to hand when completing other exercises.

Tip: The acronyms contained in the sequence are there to aid memory. If your client wishes to change them (to make them more memorable for themselves) that is acceptable just as long as the *meaning* of the step is not altered.

At this stage, the idea of this exercise is to introduce the sequence. There should be no expectation for the client to memorise or indeed understand the whole sequence. The subsequent exercises in this workbook explore each of the stages, and Exercise 11 reviews the sequence as a whole again.

Note: Provide encouragement to your client at this stage that they *will* be able to 'do' the sequence by the end of the workbook. Do not allow them to leave this session feeling there is an unachievable goal ahead of them.

Step 1: As with exercise 1, show the client the sequence on worksheet 2(a) and explain that the exercises in this workbook are based on exploring and expanding the steps of the sequence.

Step 2: Ask the client to provide a non-offending related potential problem, such as 'how to get home'.

Step 3: Using a flipchart sheet, work the problem provided into the steps of the sequence, an example for the problem above is provided for illustration purposes on worksheet 2(b) where all the steps for 'how to get home?' are broken down.

Note: This step/exercise relies heavily on the practitioner to support the client. There is *no* expectation for the offender to know any of the sequence but allow them to participate and provide answers as appropriate to their *current* level of understanding.

Exercise 2 – Worksheet 2(a)

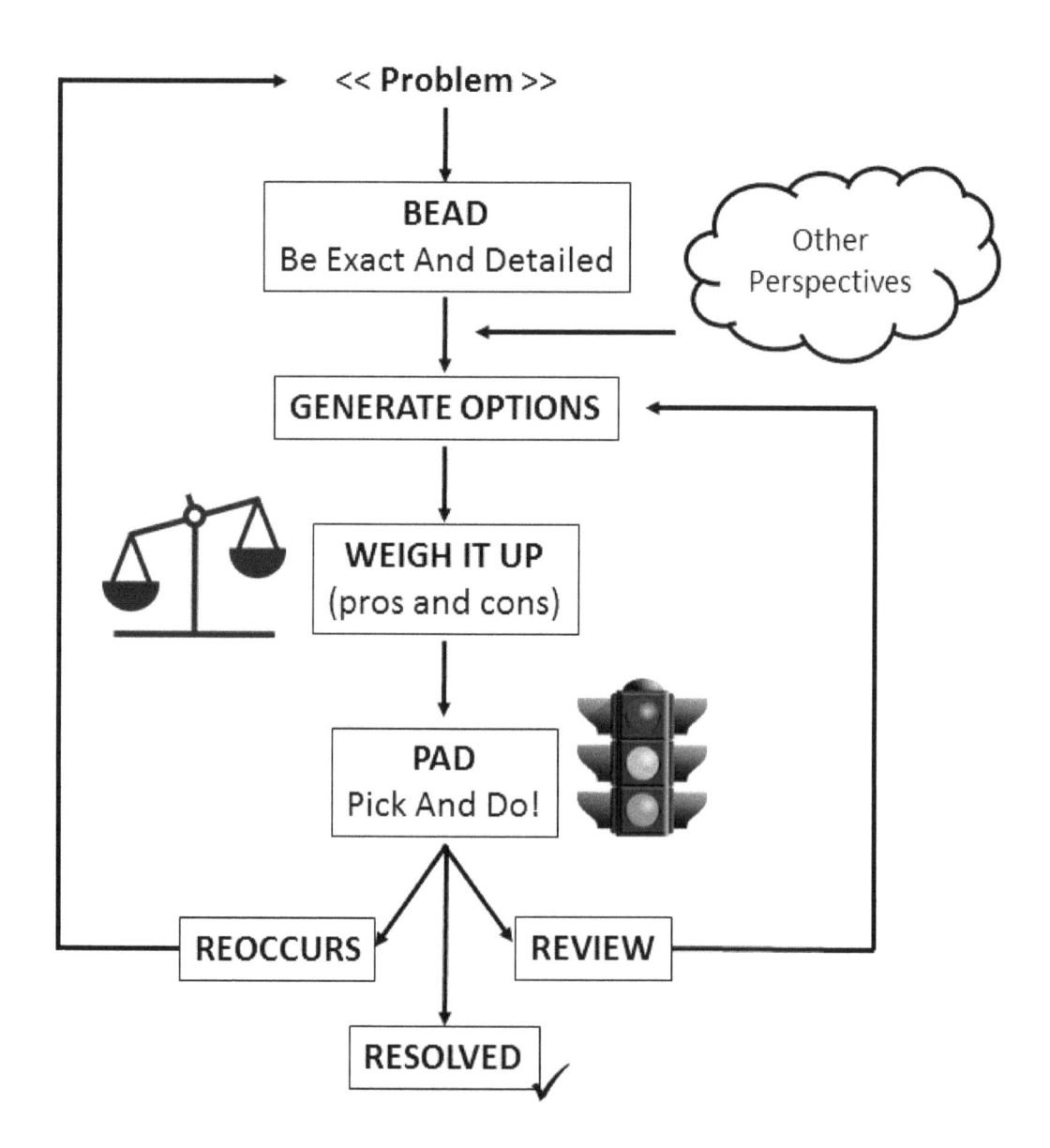

```
                    << Problem >>
                          │
                          ▼
              ┌───────────────────────┐          ╭─────────────╮
              │        BEAD           │         (   Other       )
              │  Be Exact And Detailed│◄────────(  Perspectives )
              └───────────────────────┘          ╰─────────────╯
                          │
                          ▼
              ┌───────────────────────┐
      ⚖       │   GENERATE OPTIONS    │◄──────────┐
              └───────────────────────┘           │
                          │                       │
                          ▼                       │
              ┌───────────────────────┐           │
              │     WEIGH IT UP       │           │
              │   (pros and cons)     │           │
              └───────────────────────┘           │
                          │                       │
                          ▼                       │
              ┌───────────────────────┐  🚦       │
              │        PAD            │           │
              │     Pick And Do!      │           │
              └───────────────────────┘           │
                      ↙    ↓    ↘                 │
              ┌──────────┐  │  ┌──────────┐       │
              │ REOCCURS │  │  │  REVIEW  │───────┘
              └──────────┘  │  └──────────┘
                   │        ▼
                   │  ┌──────────┐
                   │  │ RESOLVED │ ✓
                   │  └──────────┘
                   └──► (back to Problem)
```

32

Exercise 2 – Worksheet 2(b)

The problem is – *how to get home?*

BEAD – I have no money for a taxi or bus. My home is over 6 miles away so I don't feel I can walk. My bicycle was stolen last week. There is no train station near my home.

Other perspectives – some people may feel that 6 miles is walkable. Some people may say I should have planned my return before I set out.

Generate options – I could hitchhike. I could call a friend/my mum and ask for a lift. I could ask the Probation Officer for a travel warrant. I could walk.

Weigh it up –

	PROS	**CONS**
Hitchhike	free, quick	dangerous, unreliable
Call a friend	free, quick, safe	asking for a favour again, might need to offer petrol money
Call Mum	free, quick, safe	Mum will moan, may have to do some chores to make up for the journey
Travel warrant	free	buses are infrequent, it's raining
Walk	free	it's a long way, I don't have suitable shoes on

Look at what means the most to me in terms of pros and cons; where do I place most value, what are the short and long term consequences of each action (the 'how' of doing these steps are expanded in exercises 6 and 8)

PAD – call a friend

3 R's – try calling a friend but he doesn't answer. This option needs to be *'reviewed'*, so look back at my options and decide to try calling mum. She answers and agrees, and the problem is *resolved*!

3 R's explained

Reoccurs – After going through the sequence and trying an option, the same problem reoccurs. Go back to the start of the sequence to look at what went wrong, and work back through the sequence with more detail.

Review – Having picked an option, it almost solves the problem but not quite… Go back to the generating options stage, *review* the choices and pick another option.

Resolved – An option is identified, tried, and it satisfactorily solves the problem!

Exercise 2a – Alternative Exercise

The actual sequence to the exercise is a critical part of this workbook, in terms of the practitioner relating it to the other exercises and the client being able to follow it when confronted by a problem in order to work to a satisfactory resolution. However, depending on the learning style of the client, it may be beneficial to alter the methodology of the exercise. Below is an example of a presentation adjustment for a client who presents as a kinaesthetic learner.

Step 1: Cut out the elements to the exercise, along the dotted lines, before meeting with the client.

Step 2: On a flipchart sheet write 'problem' at the top and 'solution' at the bottom. Discuss with the offender what steps they think they may be able to take in order to join the two statements. Allow the offender to write and scribble ideas, if literacy skills allow.

Step 3: Once the offender has completed Step 2, give them the sequence pieces and ask them to reassemble the 'puzzle'. Assist at the minimum level possible.

Step 4: Discuss the offender's assembled sequence compared to the one from this workbook; where are the differences and why?

Note: Just because there may be a difference in the offender's sequence to the one in this workbook does not make their sequence invalid. The difference may highlight how an offender is processing information. Further, the sequence in this workbook is specifically designed to be simplistic to aid memorisation.

Exercise 2a – Worksheet

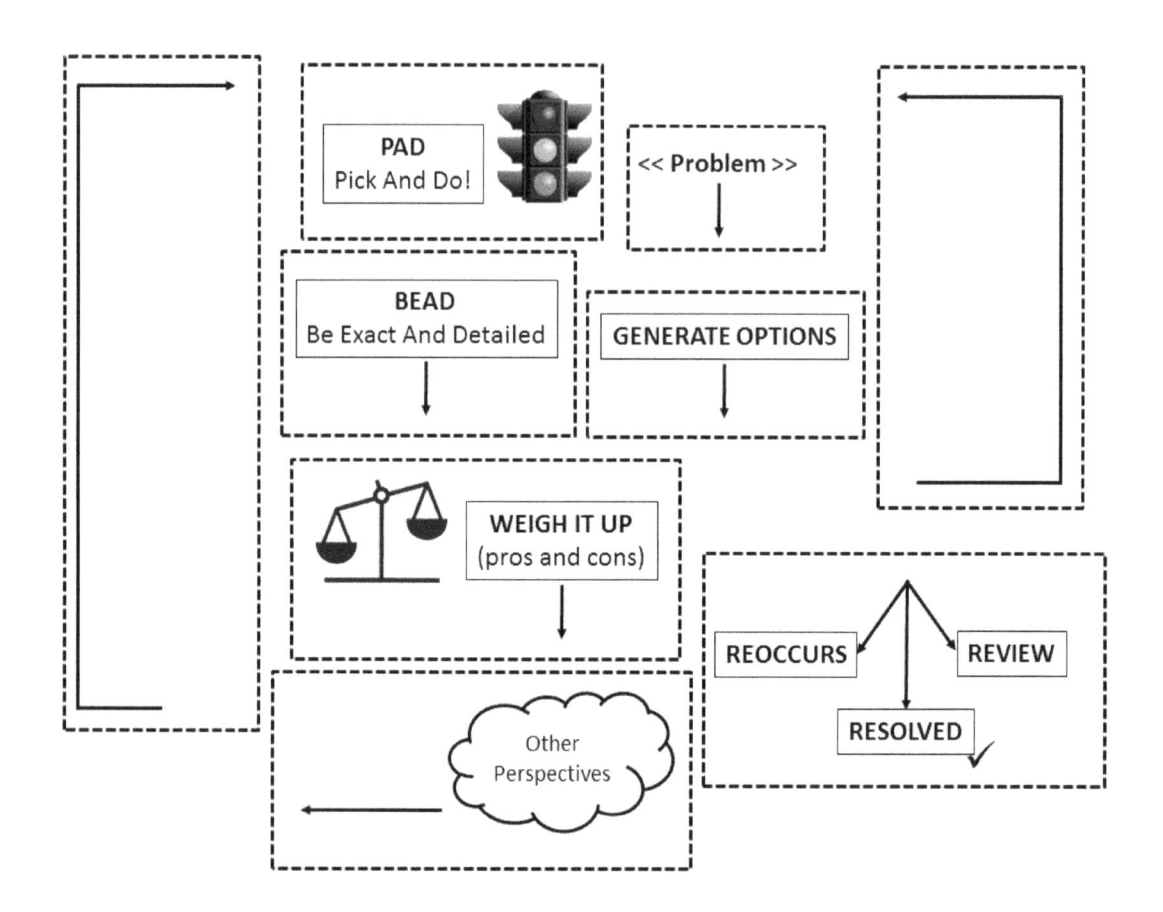

- **PAD** — Pick And Do!
- **<< Problem >>**
- **BEAD** — Be Exact And Detailed
- **GENERATE OPTIONS**
- **WEIGH IT UP** (pros and cons)
- Other Perspectives
- REOCCURS / REVIEW / RESOLVED

Exercise 2 – Out of Session Work

At this stage, the aim of the work is to increase an offender's awareness of the consequences of behaviour and decision making.

Step 1: Provide the offender with the out of session worksheet and explain to them that they need to complete it between sessions. Explain that they need to find at least one example of a problem which is not satisfactorily resolved, either for the primary person concerned or because of the consequences on people around that person. The scenario does not have to be one they have experienced directly and it may even come from a television programme if appropriate.

Step 2: Once an appropriate example has been found, the offender needs to consider where on the sequence the person concerned 'went wrong' and then rework the scenario to create a better potential outcome.

Tip: Encourage the offender to use the 'trigger triangle' if they struggle to identify either what went wrong or how to change it.

Step 3: Review the completed worksheet with the offender at the next session.

Exercise 2 – Out of Session Worksheet

The problem solving sequence:

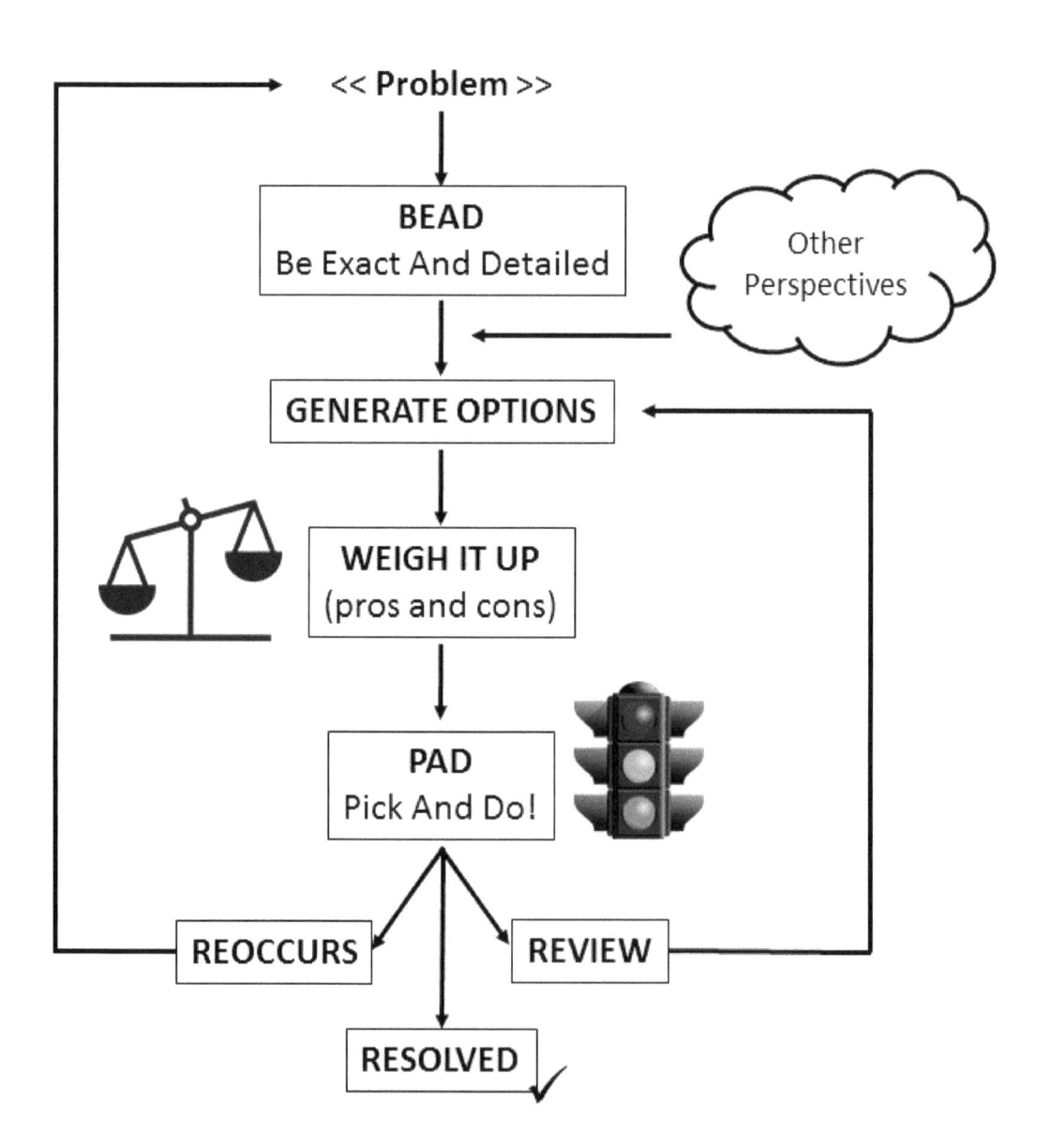

<< **Problem** >>

↓

BEAD
Be Exact And Detailed

Other Perspectives

↓

GENERATE OPTIONS

↓

WEIGH IT UP
(pros and cons)

↓

PAD
Pick And Do!

↓

REOCCURS — **REVIEW**

↓

RESOLVED ✓

Exercise 2 – Out of Session Worksheet

Describe the problem scenario:

Why did it 'go wrong'?

At what stage did the person concerned 'leave' the problem solving sequence?

How would you rectify this (put it right)?

Exercise 2 – Review

Name at least one thing that has been learned from this exercise.

Additional Notes:

Exercise 3 – Defining a Problem

Category of exercise: Defining problems.

> **Tutor Notes:**
>
> In order to tackle or address a problem, we need to know what it is first. If we do not know what the problem is exactly, then how can we ever solve it to the fullest extent? Whilst identifying a problem may sound simple, it is possibly the hardest element of problem solving - on a practical level. This is because the person with the problem sometimes does not want to accept that there is *any* problem, or sometimes the person does not consider that there are problematic parts to their behaviour, or even which part of the behaviour is the problematic part! Defining the problem can be a very confusing thing.
>
> In this exercise, we suggest a process that can be used to help the client identify what the problem is exactly. Therefore, the 'criteria' for the client undertaking this exercise is that they acknowledge that some behaviour in their life that is a problem, even if they cannot seem to pinpoint what it is. For example, they have reached the contemplation stage (see section one) of the cycle of change in that they do not want to continue to commit offences but are unsure how to action this.
>
> *Note*: Should the client not consider their behaviour to be problematic, then it is worth starting on the consequential thinking exercise (Exercise 8) first, and then returning to do this exercise.
>
> When completing this exercise, you will notice that there are two different worksheets. The first worksheet helps the client identify what other people's problems are, and the next worksheet looks at what the client's problems are. Once this is completed, the problems are changed into treatment goals and should be revisited upon completion of this workbook.

Step 1: Read out, or ask the client to read out, the three scenarios on the worksheet (3a).

Step 2: Ask the client to consider what the problem is, for each scenario, and then complete the sentence underneath the scenario which looks at identifying the specific problem in that situation.

Step 3: The tutor should discuss with the client how easy or difficult step 2 was, as well as potential different perspectives, and why there may be more than one problem in each scenario; for example, one problem may be that the client does not 'see' a problem.

Step 4: The tutor should tell the client that they are now going to look at their (the client's) problems and the tutor should ask the client to answer yes or no to the statements in the questionnaire. If the client answers yes to any of the questions, then the client should explain clearly what this problem is - by completing the sentence underneath (Worksheet 3b)

Step 5: The tutor should ask the client to consider a maximum of three problems, ideally the most prominent or critical ones in their life at the current time. From these the client should identify how they are going to address them and within what timescale. These will then be the 'treatment goals' which should be revisited at the end of the workbook (assuming the exercises are used in sequence). If not, agree a time frame when the goals will be revisited.

Exercise 3 – Worksheet 3(a)

Read the following three scenarios and then complete the sentence exploring what the problem is - for each situation.

Scenario (a)

In an interview with his key worker, Jack said that he feels as though he is struggling and that everything is getting on top of him. When the key worker asked Jack why, he said that he did not know. However Jack went on to talk about never having enough money because he is unemployed and that this is getting him down.

Complete the following sentence:

Jack's problem is..

Scenario (b)

Jane is arguing a lot with her sister. Jane wants her own bedroom, but she does not want to tell her mum as she thinks this will make her mum stressed, and make her feel like their house is not big enough.

Complete the following sentence:

Jane's problem is..

Scenario (c)

Max has to go to the Probation Service every week. If Max misses an appointment, he will get a warning from his Probation Officer who Max meets with when he visits. Max went along to his weekly session late on one occasion and was asked 'why' by the Probation Officer. Max became upset as he felt that he had made an extra effort that week because he had given up an opportunity to go away with his friends for the day. Max decided that he does not like his Probation Officer and so he makes excuses for not coming in for his appointments. Max then gets sent back to Prison for not keeping his Probation appointments.

Complete the following sentence:

Max's problem is..

Exercise 3 – Worksheet 3(b)

Answer the following:

Thinking about your life, answer yes or no to the following statements. If you answer yes to any of the statements try to explain it by completing a sentence underneath.

Accommodation is a problem for me   YES   NO

My problem with accommodation is:

Education is a problem for me   YES   NO

My problem with education is:

Employment is a problem for me   YES   NO

My problem with employment is:

Finances are a problem for me   YES   NO

My problem with finances are:

Making decisions is a problem for me   YES   NO

My problem with making decisions is:

My health is a problem for me   YES   NO

My problem with my health is:

I do not think before I act   YES   NO

My problem here is:

Anger management is a problem for me   YES   NO

My problem with anger is:

Alcohol is a problem for me   YES   NO

My problem with alcohol is:

Drugs are a problem for me   YES   NO

My problem with drugs is:

Looking at the answers you have given, turn a maximum of three of your problems into aims / goals by completing the following sentence:

GOAL NUMBER ONE

My problem is:

My aim / goal therefore is to:

I will do this by (timescale):_____

GOAL NUMBER TWO

My problem is:

My aim / goal therefore is to:

I will do this by (timescale):_____

GOAL NUMBER THREE

My problem is:

My aim / goal therefore is to:

I will do this by (timescale):_____

Exercise 3 – Alternative Exercise

The questionnaire relating to the problems the client feels they have (and don't have) at the present time still needs to be completed. This is because even if they do not admit to the practitioner that they have a problem, they may have 'registered' it in their own mind as being something they need to solve. This internal acknowledgement can be part of the transfer from pre contemplative to contemplative (see section one).

Step 1: Cut out the two spinners on the worksheet and poke a pencil through the centre hole.

Step 2: Ask the client to spin both spinners and read out the results for spinner one then spinner two. This should create a sentence along the lines of 'The problem for *Anna the shopkeeper* was that *the spanner was the wrong size*'.

Step 3: Discuss with the offender whether the sentence is correct and under what circumstances it may be correct or incorrect. So for the example above, it would initially appear that the sentence does not make sense, as a shopkeeper is not a mechanic. However, if Anna was attempting to put some new display shelves together, the problem may become apparent.

Step 4: Try and agree a definition of a 'problem' with the client, along the lines of:

1. A matter or situation regarded as unwelcome or harmful and needing to be dealt with and overcome.
2. A thing difficult to achieve or accomplish.   (OED 2012)

Exercise 3a - Worksheet

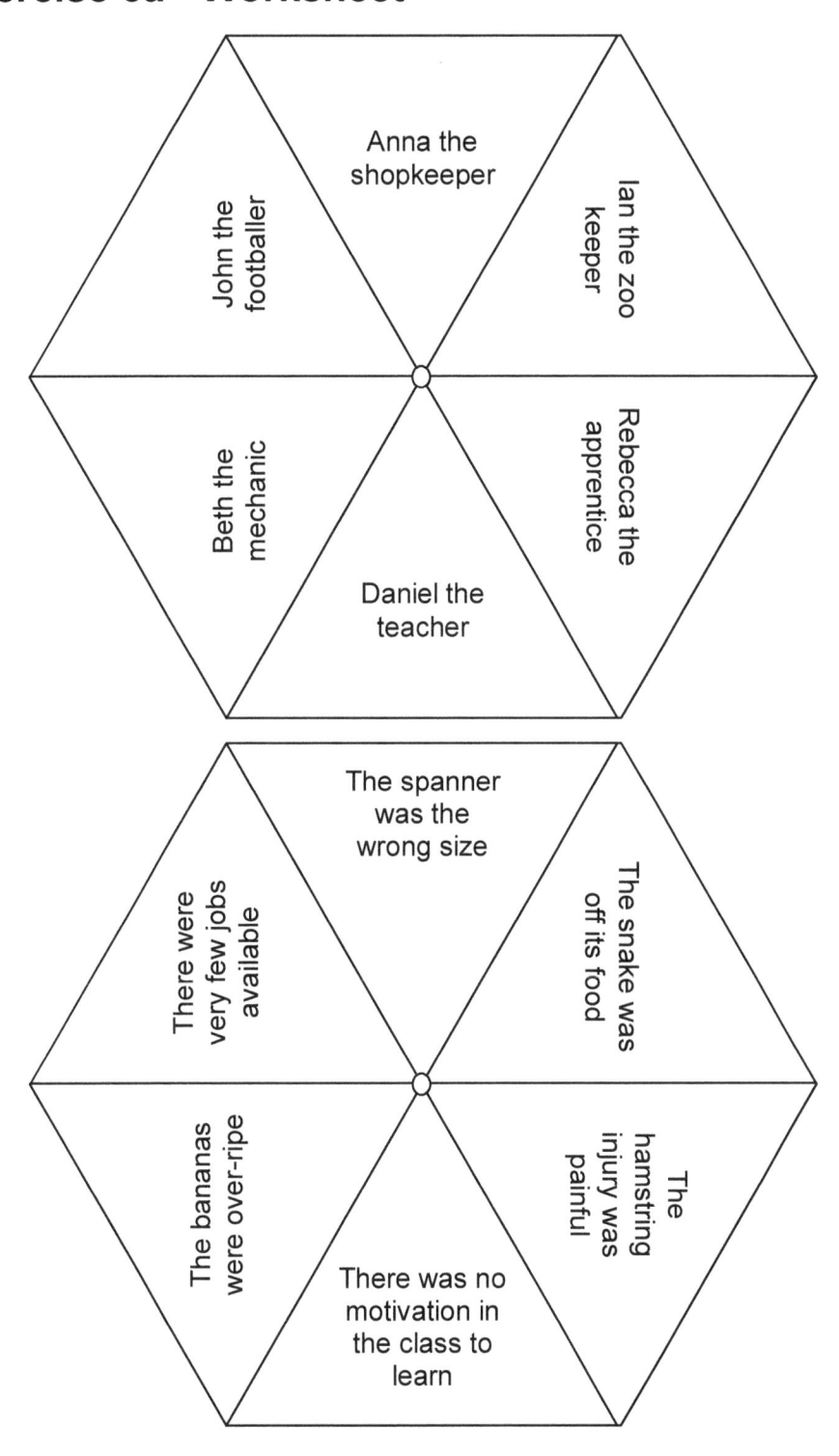

Hexagon 1:
- Anna the shopkeeper
- Ian the zoo keeper
- Rebecca the apprentice
- Daniel the teacher
- Beth the mechanic
- John the footballer

Hexagon 2:
- The spanner was the wrong size
- The snake was off its food
- The hamstring injury was painful
- There was no motivation in the class to learn
- The bananas were over-ripe
- There were very few jobs available

Exercise 3 – Out of Session Work

As out of session work, the facilitator should ask the client to consider one area in their life that they would like to change or consider improving. This simple question is aimed at encouraging the client to begin *reflecting* on the different areas of their life. The skill of reflection is an important one in that by being aware of our actions, the consequences and areas we may want to change, we can address matters before they become problematic. Reflection is covered as an exercise in itself in exercise 12.

Reflection for out of session work can be supported by completing the out of session work questionnaire. The facilitator should explain to the client that the worksheet asks the respondent 'Why they would like to improve or change this area?' and 'If it has ever caused them problems?'(either with the law or in life generally). It then asks them to change the identified problem into a goal they would like to achieve - thus finishing on a positive note.

Exercise 3 – Out of Session Work Worksheet

Please answer in the boxes provided

The area I would like to change or improve is:

The reason I would like to change is:

This area has caused me problems by...

Now reword the information above into a positive goal!

Exercise 3 – Review

Name at least one thing that has been learned from this exercise.

Additional Notes:

Exercise 4 – Being Exact

Category of exercise: Defining problems.

Tutor notes

Where a deficit in thinking skills or consequential thinking has been identified as a problem, the aim of the practitioner will be to increase a client's ability in these areas; to allow them to change *their* own behaviour as a result of changing *their* thinking and subsequent decision making. In order for an offender to begin to *want* to change their behaviour, they first need to be able to recognise and understand the problem.

Having a 'problem' can seem rather daunting and insurmountable. The purpose of this exercise is firstly to allow the offender to boil the problem down into constituent, and importantly, achievable parts. The simpler the problem appears, the more motivation to tackle it can be garnered. Even where the actual 'putting it in to practice part' may be difficult, the motivation to try is at least present.

Step 1: Explain to the offender that the purpose of this exercise is to whittle down the big 'problem' of offending (or problem behaviour) to a simpler more understandable one. Use the worksheet on page 55, starting at the top of the arrow where the problem 'offending' has already been written; if applicable, the type of offending can also be added, such as 'offending: thefts'.

Step 2: Ask the offender to state why they offend and add the answer to the next rung down on the arrow.

Step 3: Continue to ask the offender 'why' to their answer, adding their answers to the arrows in sequence, until they reach an absolute statement.

Here is an example:

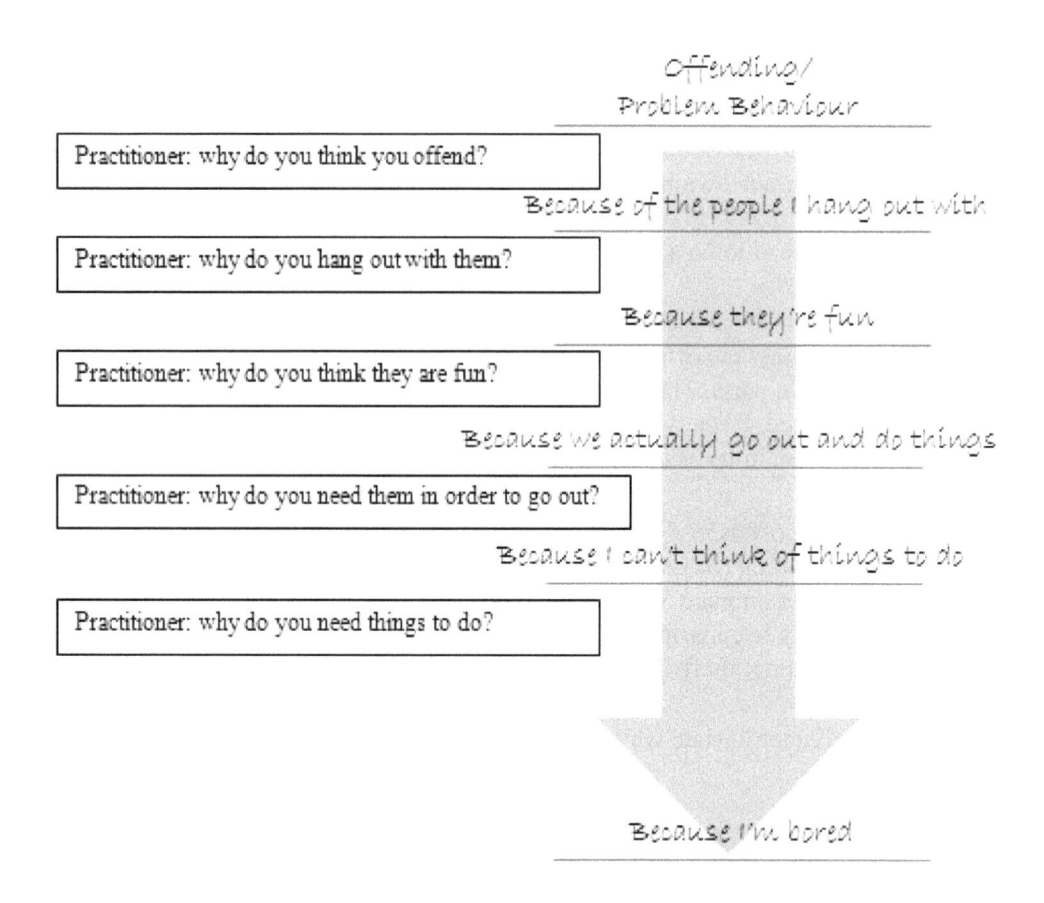

```
                                          Offending/
                                          Problem Behaviour
┌──────────────────────────────────────┐
│ Practitioner: why do you think you offend? │
└──────────────────────────────────────┘
                          Because of the people I hang out with
┌──────────────────────────────────────┐
│ Practitioner: why do you hang out with them? │
└──────────────────────────────────────┘
                          Because they're fun
┌──────────────────────────────────────┐
│ Practitioner: why do you think they are fun? │
└──────────────────────────────────────┘
                          Because we actually go out and do things
┌──────────────────────────────────────┐
│ Practitioner: why do you need them in order to go out? │
└──────────────────────────────────────┘
                          Because I can't think of things to do
┌──────────────────────────────────────┐
│ Practitioner: why do you need things to do? │
└──────────────────────────────────────┘
                                    ↓
                          Because I'm bored
```

Note: The final answer here 'I'm bored' is identifiable as 'the end' since the next question from the practitioner ('why are you bored?') is likely to lead to an answer which has been given previously, namely 'because I can't think of things to do'. There is little point in going around in circles such as this, even if the practitioner feels there is a futher layer to break down. Remember, roll with resistance (see section one).

Step 4: Explain to the offender that they have now identified the main crux of their motivation to offend, and they will be able to work on strategies to combat this during the next sessions.

Step 5: Explain to the offender that the 'exact' part comes from the last line but the 'detailed' part is all the lines above, as in: 'being bored is a problem because I can't think of things to do on my own, and when I have fun with the people I like to hang out with - I tend to offend'.

Exercise 4 - Worksheet

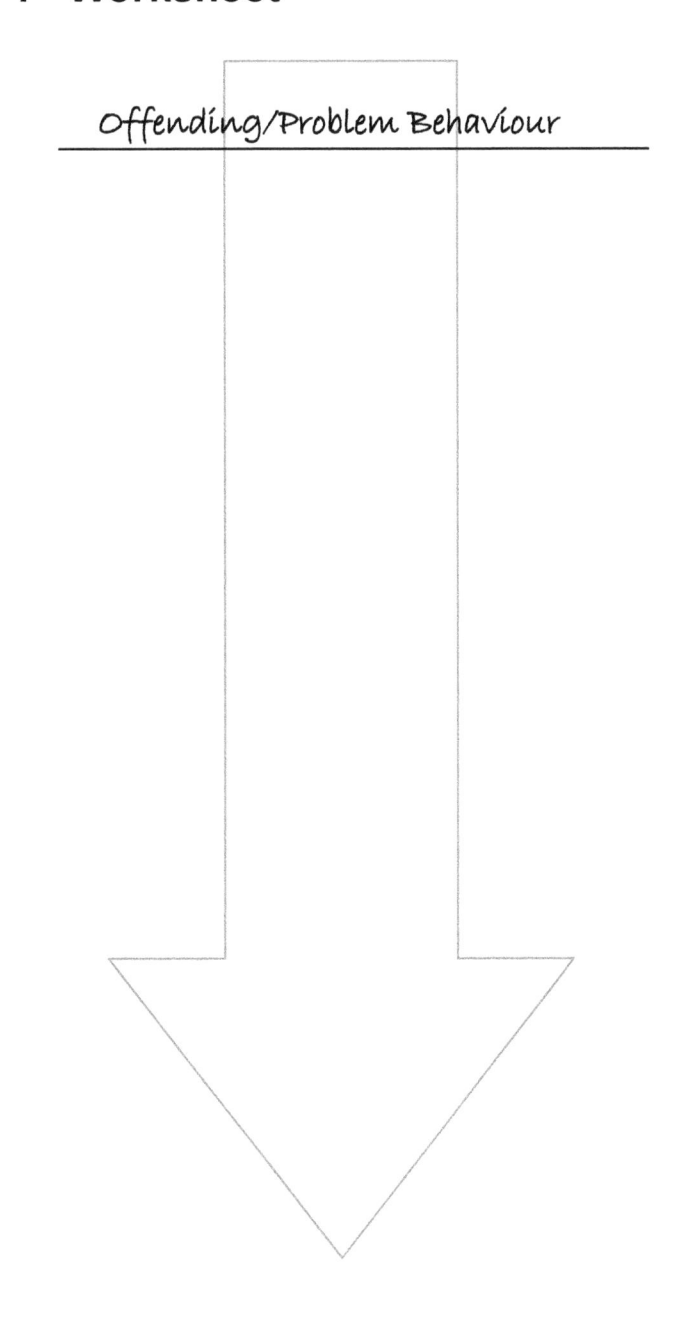

Offending/Problem Behaviour

Exercise 4a – Alternative Exercise

Step 1: Explain to the offender that the idea of this exercise is similar to darts in that they need to score as many points as possible within one go. They have as many darts (or attempts) as they want. Each connected segment is worth 10 points. Use a pen as the 'dart' to mark each segment that is 'hit'.

Step 2: Use the completed dartboard first and ask the offender to use their darts to mark as many of the statements as they can in the segments. Start at the bulls-eye and end at one of the outer segments. The client can mark as many statements as they want but they *must make sense* when considered as a series of statements in answer to the question 'why'. So, for example 'why did you commit that theft?', *'because…'*, 'and why was that?', *'because…'* and so on.

Step 3: Provide the blank copy of the target and ask the offender to complete it for their own offending or problem this time. Start at the bulls-eye again and write either the offence type, or just the word 'offending', or the problem they are currently facing in the centre.

Step 4: As with exercise 4, the practitioner asks 'why is this a problem?' and the answer is written in another segment. Then the practitioner asks 'why' again. Continue until an outer segment is reached and can be completed with the absolute statement (see exercise 4 for an example).

Tip: The route taken from the centre can be a direct straight line or go round in circles. The more segments used, however, the more points (and detail) the offender will have.

Step 5: The more segments (more detailed) an offender can complete, the higher they 'score'. Explain to the offender that, in terms of 'being exact and detailed' in problem solving, the 'exact' part comes from the outer segment but the 'detailed' part is all other segments.

Exercise 4a – Worksheet

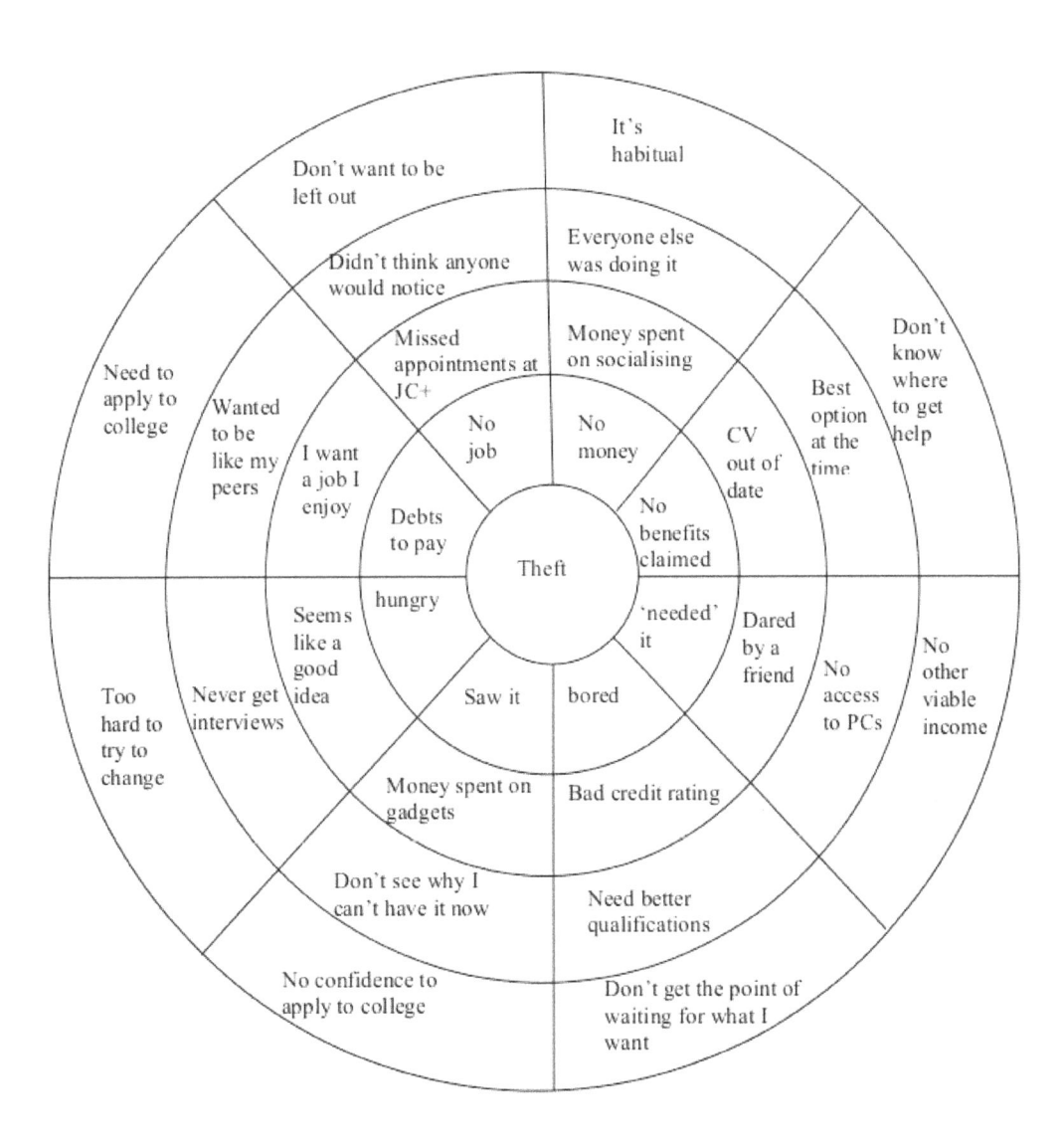

Concentric circle diagram centered on "Theft":

Inner ring (around Theft): No job; No money; CV out of date; No benefits claimed; 'needed' it; bored; Saw it; hungry; Debts to pay; I want a job I enjoy

Middle ring: Missed appointments at JC+; Money spent on socialising; Best option at the time; Dared by a friend; No access to PCs; Bad credit rating; Money spent on gadgets; Seems like a good idea; Never get interviews; Wanted to be like my peers

Outer ring: Don't want to be left out; It's habitual; Everyone else was doing it; Didn't think anyone would notice; Don't know where to get help; No other viable income; Need better qualifications; Don't get the point of waiting for what I want; No confidence to apply to college; Don't see why I can't have it now; Too hard to try to change; Need to apply to college

Exercise 4a – Worksheet

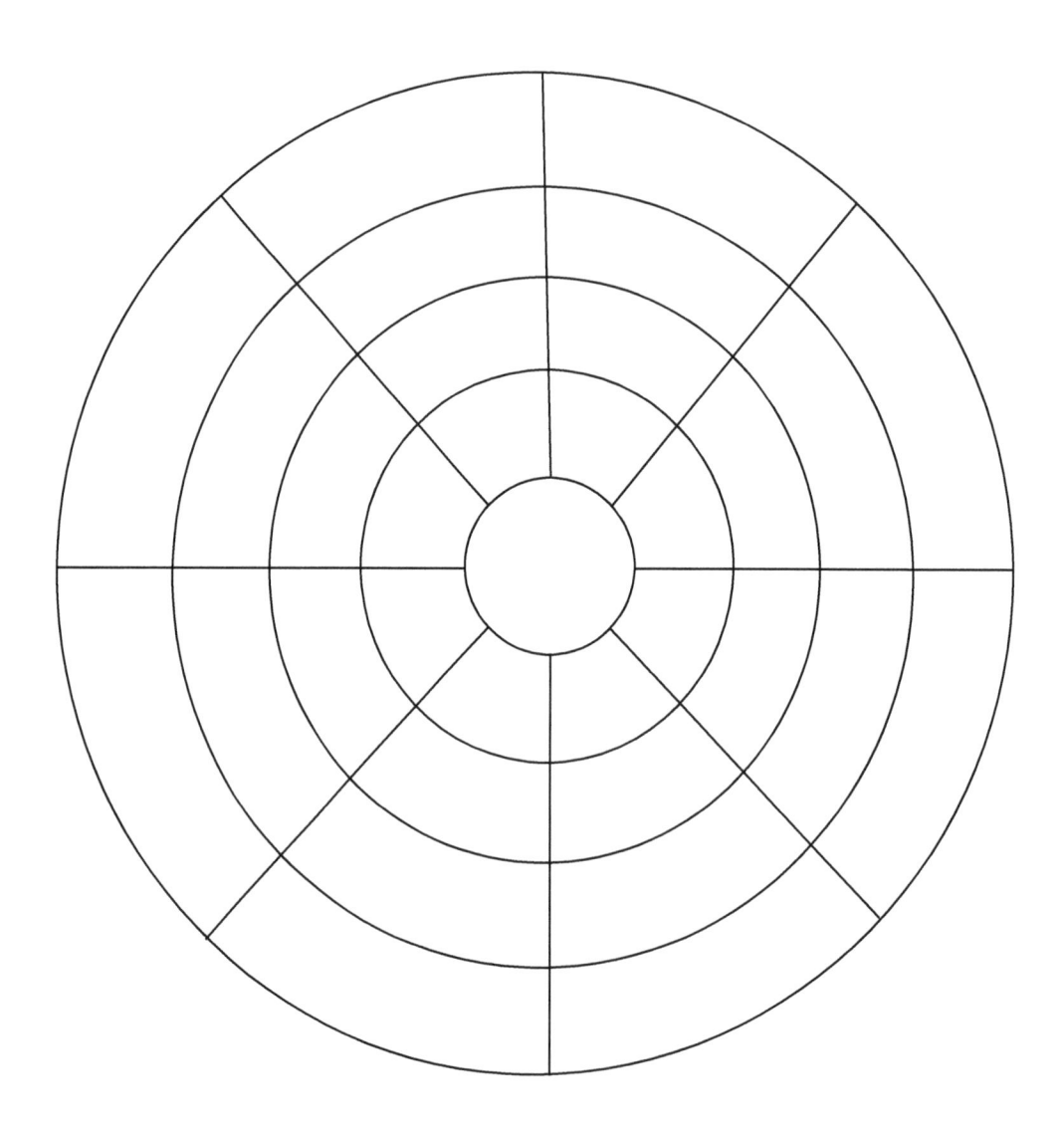

Exercise 4 – Out of Session Work

Being exact in the context of this workbook refers to getting to the hub of exactly what is wrong, and getting there by going through the *reasons* (details) as to why that problem exists. The idea can be likened to ingredients combining to make a meal – the ingredients are the details and the meal is the resultant 'problem'.

The out of session work requires the client to write a 'recipe for disaster'. Any disaster is suitable from the extinction of the dinosaurs to their football team being kicked out of the Premier League.

Explain the concepts to the client as described above, and support them in choosing a disaster. Explain that they need to write all the ingredients for that disaster in as many steps/detail as possible. Provide the worksheet if appropriate.

Exercise 4 – Out of Session Worksheet

Write the 'disaster' in the explosion and the contributing factors (reasons) in the arrows.

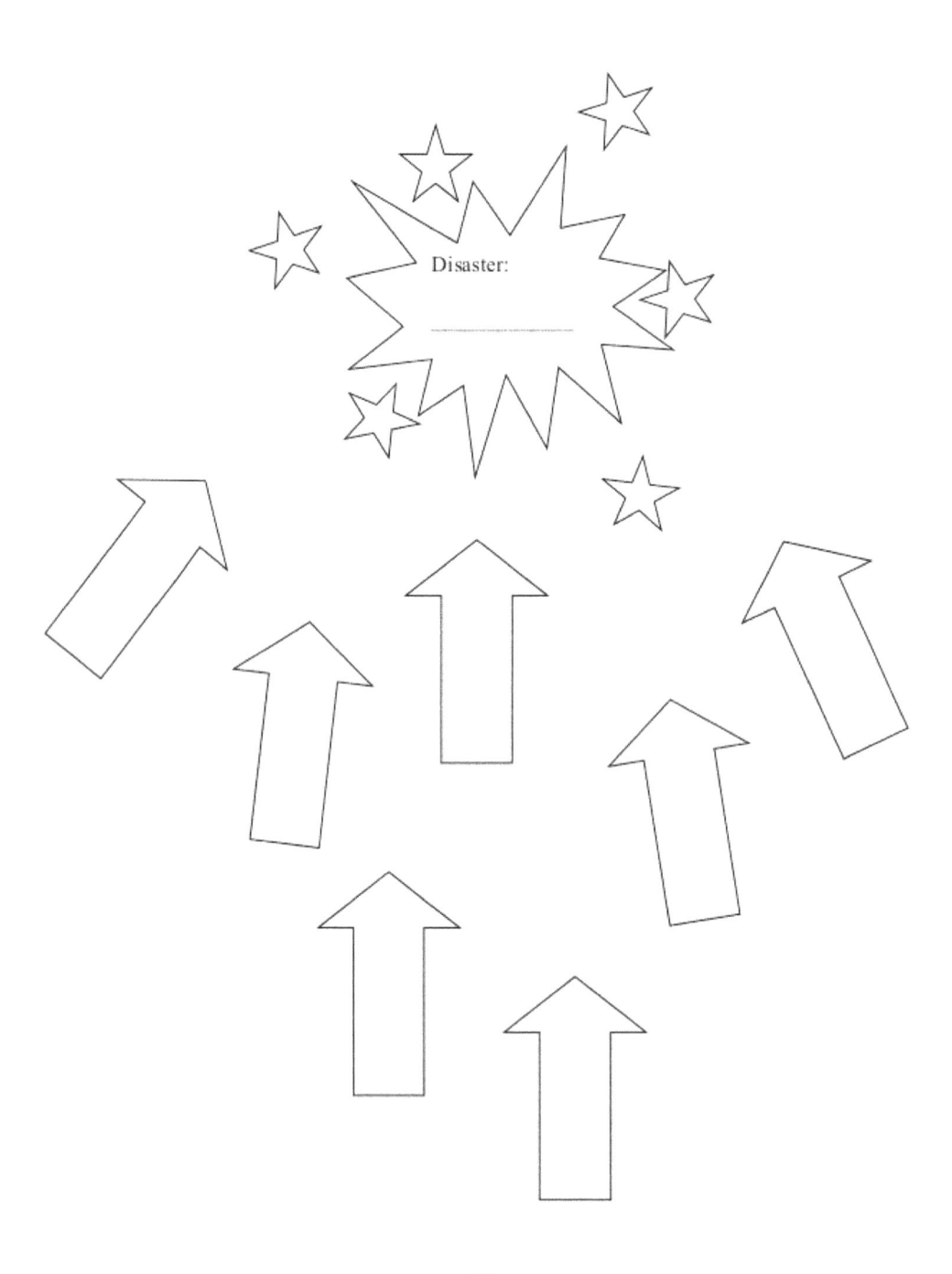

Disaster: _____

Exercise 4 – Review

Name at least one thing that has been learned from this exercise.

Additional Notes:

Exercise 5 – Brain Storming Exercise

Category of exercise: Generating options

Tutor Notes

Here the tutor will be seeking to help the offender understand how to generate relevant options to solve their problems.

In order to undertake this exercise, it is important to focus on using an example of a problem that the client wants to solve. This exercise methodology is taken from Hussey (2012) and utilises the concept of brainstorming.

Step 1: Explain that the client will now be completing an exercise focused on generating options for any problem that they want to solve, or want to discuss.

Step 2: Explain that this exercise is called "brainstorming". The idea being to simply generate lots of alternatives for an idea. The tutor should also explain that no answer is wrong but challenge any inappropriate comments.

Tip: Try to *sell* this exercise as being about learning to generate lots of different possible solutions for any given problem.

Step 3: Use the worksheet for this exercise. Ask the client to think about their problem, and consider as many solutions as possible to solve the problem. When the client answers, the tutor should draw a line from the statement in the circle with the answer at the end. For example:

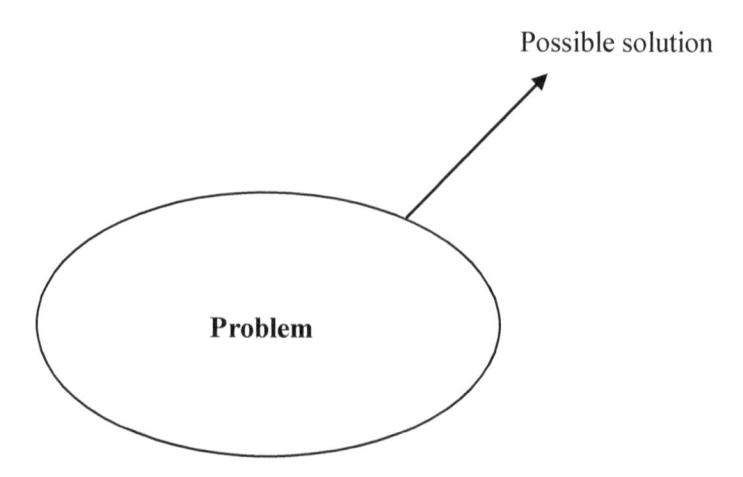

Possible solution

Problem

Tip: If the client struggles, get them to consider the details (see exercise 4) of the problem and look at solving the 'big' problem by addressing the smaller parts in turn.

Exercise 5 – Worksheet

Put your problem in the middle and generate as many possible solutions as you can think of:

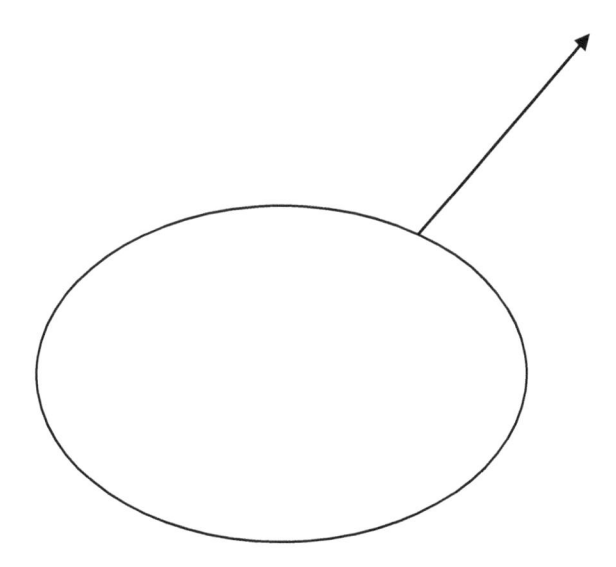

Exercise 5 – Alternative Exercise

This alternative exercise is set in the style of a game show and should be fun for both the practitioner and the offender. Having fun is a good method of learning but it is the responsibility of the practitioner to ensure that the learning points are revised and understood at the end of the session. In this case, the learning point is: the more choice that is generated, the more likely we are to arrive at the 'correct' answer.

Step 1: Cut out the three problems and all of the solution strips.

Step 2: Place all of the cards face down on the table, with the three larger problem cards at the top.

Step 3: First time round, the facilitator takes on the role of 'game show host'. Allow the offender to turn over a problem card. Either stick this card to the top of a flipchart sheet or write the problem on the top. The facilitator then picks up an answer strip *but does not show the offender*.

Step 4: The offender, knowing the problem, must try to guess the solution that the facilitator is holding. On the flip chart sheet of paper, the facilitator should write down all the possible guesses that the offender makes until they reach the right one.

Tip: If the offender struggles to guess correctly, then in true 'game show host' style, start to give clues and hints to guide them in the right direction. If this is done, then discuss afterwards with the offender that these hints were the same as the 'other perspectives' step in the problem solving sequence.

Step 5: Looking at the flipchart sheet, discuss with the offender how their guesses constitute a form of brainstorming and therefore 'generating options' also.

Step 6: Without replacing the cards already used, swap roles with the offender and play again! (The facilitator can retain the scribe role if literacy needs require this.)

Exercise 5 – Worksheet

Problem Cards

Having done the weekly supermarket shop – you get to the checkout, beep everything through - then realise you can't find your wallet	You've been watching the Sunday league football in the pouring rain – you get back to your car and can't find your keys	When taking a shortcut home through a field, you notice a large bull in one corner – you try to squeeze through a gap in the fence and get stuck

Solution Strips

Shout for help	Ask the person next to you for help	Cry	Retrace your steps	Curse
Close your eyes	Pat your pockets to look for something useful/helpful	Use your mobile to call for help	Wish you'd not gotten out of bed that morning	Hope someone notices and comes to your aid
Think of someone else to blame for your predicament	Bluff your way out of it	Get angry	Laugh	Take your clothes off
Sing loudly to make yourself feel better	Wonder if your story will make the local news	Draw a brainstorming diagram	Panic	Look for a means of escape

Exercise 5 – Out of Session Work

Should the tutor feel that more work on this topic is needed by the client then they can present optional work to be completed outside the session. Here, the client is encouraged to try to help a friend or member of their family with a problem by generating possible solutions.

Step 1: Ask the client to ask a friend or family member if they can try to help them with any problem they may want help with.

Step 2: The client uses an empty brainstorming worksheet to help the other person generate as many possible solutions as they can think of.

Step 3: The client should discuss with the tutor, during their next session, whether they managed to do this task and how it went, and also how the other person received the idea of brainstorming solutions to a problem.

Exercise 5 – Out of Session Worksheet

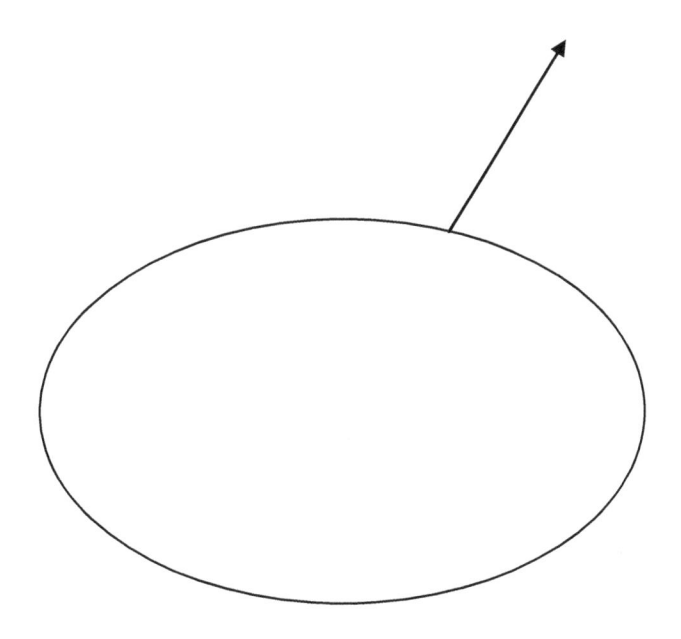

Exercise 6 – Perspective Taking

Category of exercise: Weighing up options

Tutor Notes

The next exercise looks at 'perspectives' with the client. The purpose being to stress to the client the importance of the concept that everyone can see things in a different way. This includes both what constitutes a problem, and how to solve it.

Why is perspective taking so important? If a client has completed exercise 1 they will hopefully have begun their journey into understanding how their thoughts and feelings impact on their behaviour. Now, with this in mind, it is equally important for the client to understand that people *do not* all have the same thoughts and feelings when any given situation arises. We are not all robots programmed to experience the same emotions and thoughts.

As an offender begins to understand that each person experiences different thoughts and feelings in any given situation they will then, arguably, be able to recognise that someone may have been affected by their offending behaviour and that their behaviour therefore constituted a problem. This understanding feeds in to both consequential thinking within problem solving, as well as assisting in generating options for problem solving. If you can look at a problem a different way, you may well find a different answer…

In order to achieve the aims of this exercise, the tutor needs to engage the client in what can be a rather fun exercise to facilitate.

Step 1: Explain to the client that this exercise is called the *What Can You See?* and its purpose is to explore how people can see things in different ways.

Step 2: Show the client picture 1 (below) and ask them: "What do you see?" Have fun with this exercise if you can.

Tip: It is worth explaining that there is no wrong answer for what you can see here, even (and sometimes, *especially*) if you as the tutor cannot see it.

Step 3: Replicate Step 2 with the client for picture 2, and then picture 3.

Step 4: Conclude the exercise by asking the client their thoughts about the objective of that exercise and then answer the subsequent questions.

Exercise 6 – Worksheet

Picture 1

What can you see?

Picture 2

What can you see?

Picture 3

What can you see?

Exercise 6 – Questions

Answer the following questions:

What do you think the purpose of this exercise is?

Do you think that there is a right and wrong answer to what we see in these pictures?

Why can it be helpful to look at a situation (or problem) from another angle?

Exercise 6 – Alternative Exercise

If a more kinetic exercise is required (see section one) here is an alternative exercise that can be used. It is equally fun and powerful.

Step 1: Arrange the room, prior to meeting with the offender, so that there are at least three chairs with different orientations within the room.

Step 2: Make sure that something particularly eye-catching can be seen from each chair. They should be obscured or at least not as visible from the other seating positions (the simpler the better – use a colourful poster or novelty pen on a desk, for example).

Step 3: Allow the offender to sit in any of the chairs and ask them to describe what they can see when looking forwards, then rotate to the next chair, and so on.

Step 4: Ask the offender what they think the purpose of the exercise was. Explain that the description can be brief and this part of the exercise should take no more than around ten to fifteen minutes.

Tip: If the offender has difficulty, ask them to consider how and why their answers might have varied from each chair.

Exercise 6 – Out of Session Work

Should the tutor feel that more work is needed here then they can present optional work to be completed outside the session.

Step 1: Ask the offender to find an example from one of the soaps or other popular TV programmes where the script writers have used a difference in perspectives to great effect. Preferably the example will be related to either creating or solving a problem.

Step 2: Discuss with the client what they found during the next session.

Exercise 6 – Review

Name at least one thing that has been learned from this exercise.

Additional Notes:

Exercise 7 - The Ripple Effect

Category of exercise: Weighing up options

> **Tutor Notes**
>
> In this exercise the tutor will explore what is known as the ripple effect. Namely, *when a problem is allowed to perpetuate or fester, the consequences of this can spread across the whole community.*
>
> The idea of this exercise is to try to get the offender to see and understand that any offence or behaviour impacts not only on the client and the immediate environment but other people and further afield as well. This should expand on the idea of consequential thinking which feeds in to the idea of the 'point' of working on a client's thinking skills, and the 'need' to solve problems rather than let them linger.

Step 1: Show the client the ripple diagram.

Step 2: Explain to the client how the diagram works. This being: *The offence/problem occupies the inner circle, the victim the next layer, their family the next layer, and so on, until the very outer layer is more remote such as 'government policies'.*

Note: The idea is explained as being like the impact of dropping a stone in a pond; the strongest impact is where the stone falls, but the river bank still feels the ripple and enough ripples will eventually lead to erosion.

Step 3: Ask the client to think of as many effects, as far reaching as possible, for all the elements of the circles. Try and get the offender to expand upon, and explain, each label so that for the centre circle of 'offence/problem' the immediate effect of this offence needs to be explored. For example, an offence of graffiti (indirect victim) would have an immediate impact of 'visible paint'; or an offence of robbery (direct victim) would have an immediate effect of 'creating fear for the victim' and so on. It may be that the explanation for one layer leads to the label for the next layer.

Step 4: Try and get the offender to think about why the explanation for each label may be considered a problem (it is not possible to record all of the discussion on the worksheet – simply talking about it is sufficient). So, for example, using the above impact of graffiti – visible paint – "This is a problem because ... [some people think it looks ugly]".

Tip: To engage a more resistant offender, present this exercise as a challenge to get them to think of just how far they can imagine the impact of their behaviour reaching. This approach may not be suitable in all cases and the practitioner will need to use their professional judgment. Always enable the offender to understand the negativity attached to such wide reaching consequences - the main message being that it is up to them as to whether their 'importance' to others or within society is of a negative or positive influence.

Exercise 7 – Example Diagram

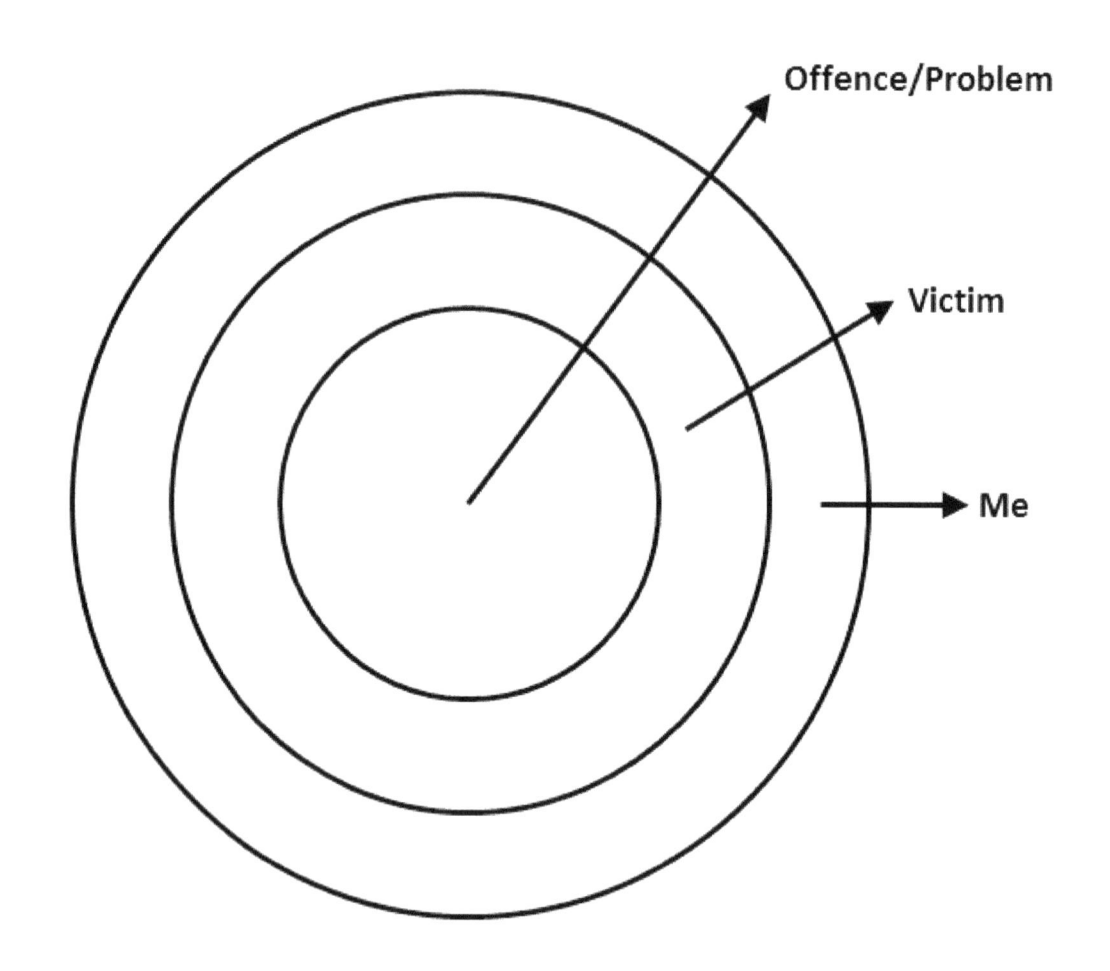

Offence/Problem

Victim

Me

Exercise 7 – Worksheet

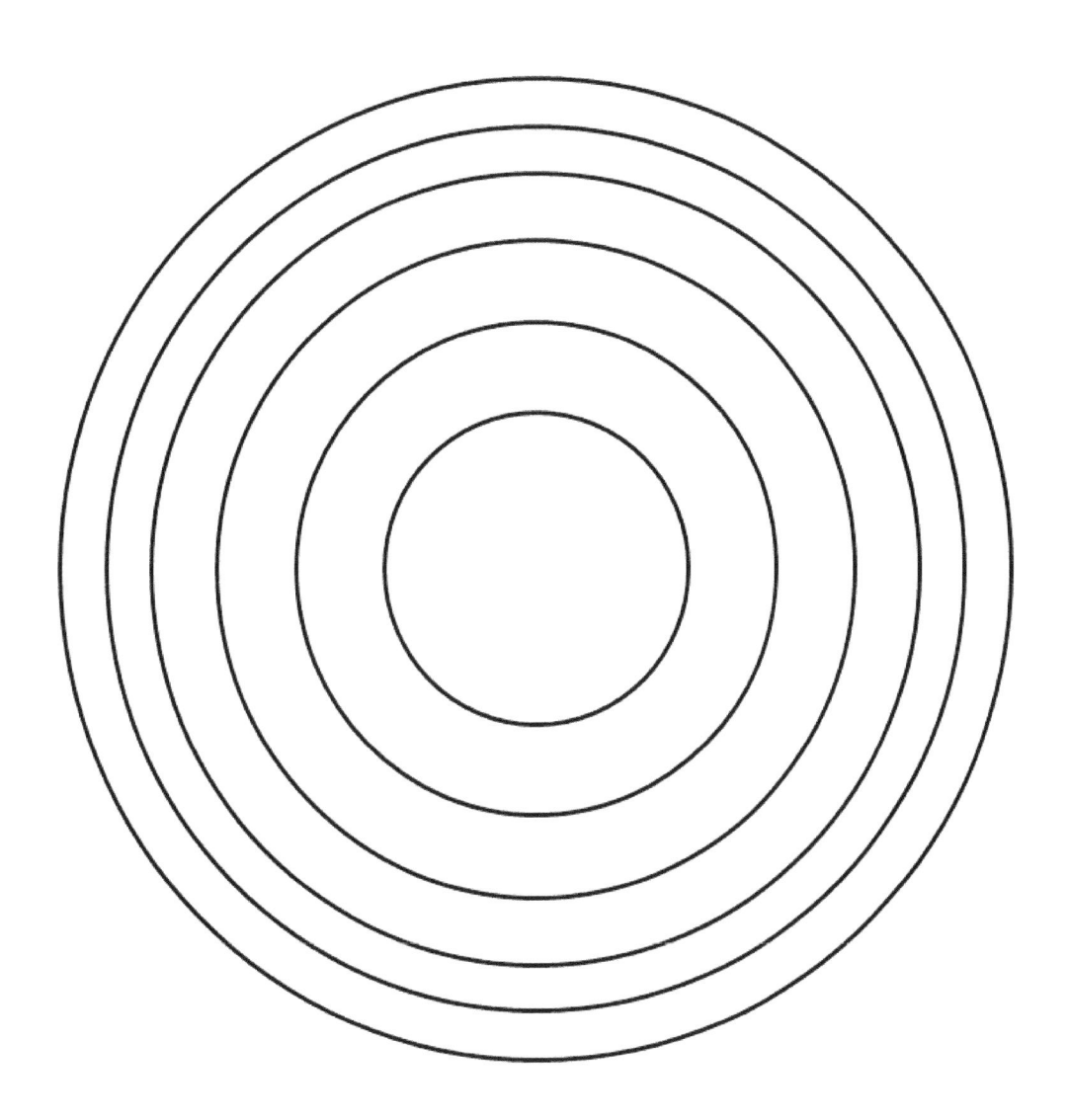

Exercise 7 – Alternative Exercise

Step 1: The tutor should clear the room of obstacles so there is a fair sized floor space available. When this is done, the tutor should lay out sections of rope or string in concentric circles (as per Worksheet 7). Try to have *at least* four circles.

Step 2: The tutor should have several cards ready, or prepare them with the offender. On each card, the facilitator or client should write the names of different people, organisations, communities, or places which could be affected by their offence or problematic behaviour.

Step 3: Ask the offender to place the cards in the circles on the floor. Here the tutor explains that the centre circle should represent the 'centre' of the issue and so people placed here feel the greatest impact from an offence. The further away from the centre, the more reduced the felt impact.

Note: The idea needs to be explained as being like the impact of dropping a stone in a pond; the strongest impact is where the stone falls, but the bank still feels the ripple and enough ripples will eventually lead to erosion.

Step 4: The facilitator should then discuss with the offender the reasons why they made the choices they did.

Note: There will always be room for debate towards the edges of the circles but challenge any answers which appear anti-social or wide of the mark such as placing the victim anywhere but the centre or first layer.

Exercise 7 – Out Of Session Work

Should the tutor feel that more work on this topic is needed by the client then they can present optional work to be completed outside the session.

Step 1: Provide the offender with a blank ripple diagram.

Step 2: Ask them to consider an event which sticks in their mind, anything from a world event to their football team scoring is appropriate.

Step 3: Get the offender to complete the ripple diagram to show both who, and how, the chosen event has impacted on the world around them.

Step 4: Review the diagram at the next session.

Exercise 7 – Out of Session Worksheet

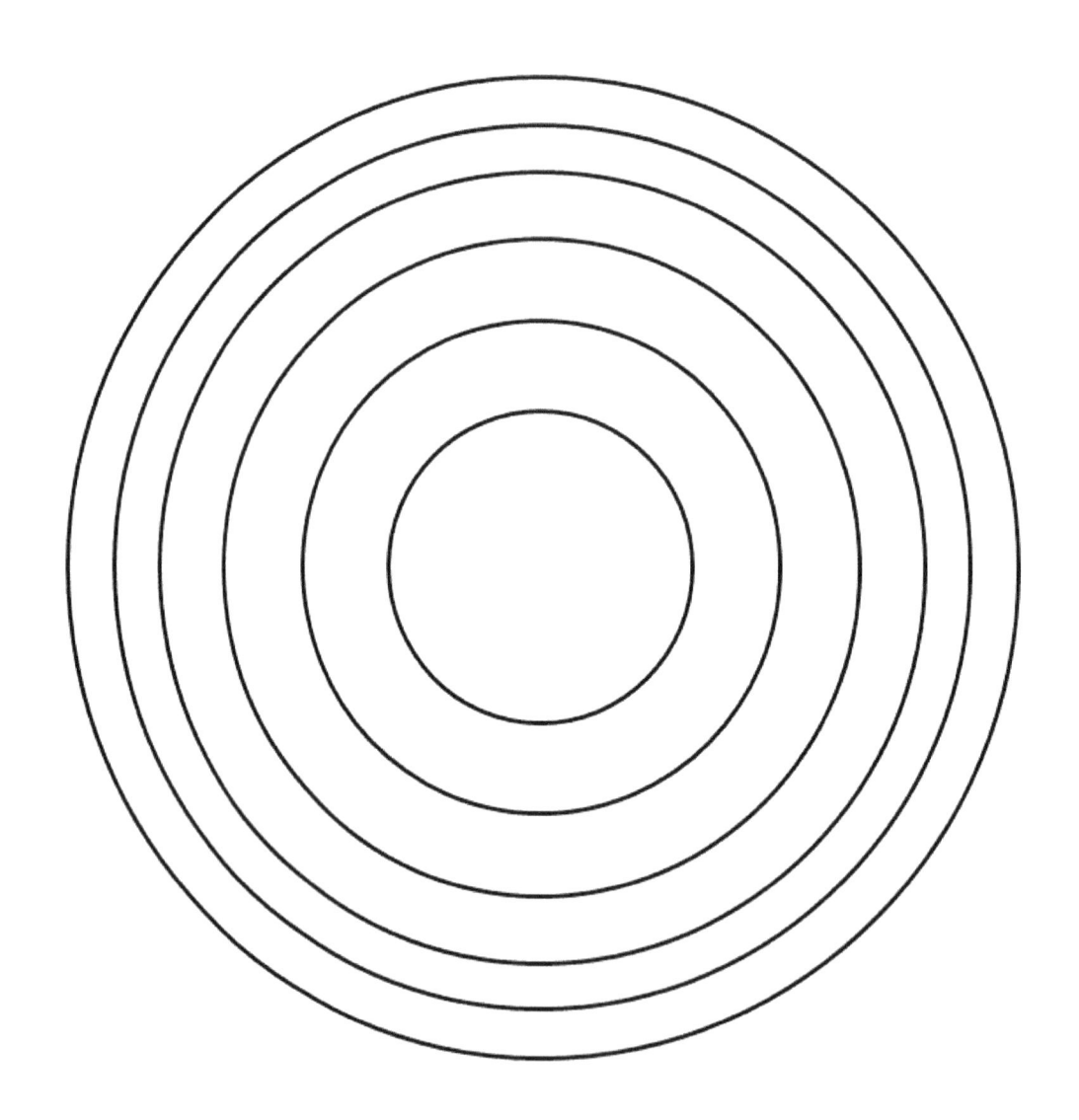

Exercise 7 – Review

Name at least one thing that has been learned from this exercise.

Additional Notes:

Exercise 8 – Consequential Thinking

Category of exercise: Weighing up options

> **Tutor Notes:**
>
> Now we have explored what options the client has, and how *other* people may view problems or solutions, the client must consider how to respond. This is, of course, down to personal choice. However, to help the client make a more informed decision, the client should consider the *consequences* of their actions. By considering the consequences the client will be able to assign a relative 'value' of positivity or negativity to each option they have generated.

To consider the consequences of behaviour, we suggest that the facilitator considers (with the client) a further brain storming exercise (see exercise 6) to help the client get to grips with this concept. However, with this exercise, we have provided various scenarios and the client should consider, if the scenario was *their* situation, what the consequences would be for *them*. There is an additional empty space available for anything the client wants to consider the consequences for. Encouragement should be made to focus on the consequences of their solution options generated in previous exercises.

Consequential thinking can be explained a little like reporting the weather. There is a lot of information available which needs to be sorted logically so that a prediction of the most likely outcome can be made. This sorting of information may be made on the basis of previous experience, on the basis of probability, or on the basis of accepting what others have said. The best predictions would contain a mixture of all three of these methods.

Step 1: Read through the first part of the information provided with the client. Ask them to highlight in three separate colours which parts of the information are 'previous experience', 'probability' and 'from others' (some pieces of information may fit into more than one category).

Note: It is important to be able to look at what category information falls into and it is just as important to look at the *reliability* of the information. Just because Granny said it, doesn't make it true…

Step 2: Read through the 'current information' section and ask the client to make a prediction about the outcome. Not all of the information in the first section will be useful for this step; sorting through information to find the relevant facts is also a skill which is required in consequential thinking.

Step 3: Repeat this for the next two sets of information.

Step 4: Remind the client to utilise the skills they have just used, and complete the brainstorming exercise.

Exercise 8 – Worksheet

Prediction One

Known information:

Red sky at night, shepherds' delight.
Red sky at morning, shepherds' warning

Thunderstorms occur when large air masses rise quickly, and ice crystals in the clouds rub against each other and cause static electricity. This electricity discharges to earth as lightning and the thunder is simply the noise.

Coming storms cause shooting corns (pain in the feet)
A sun-shiny shower won't last half an hour

Wind is caused by air moving from areas of high pressure to low pressure.

Cumulonimbus clouds are associated with thunderstorms.

The air above cities tends to be warmer than the surrounding air.

Cirrocumulus clouds look like mackerel scales and tend to predict good weather.

A cold front is caused by a cold air mass moving to a warm air mass – thunderstorms tend to be scattered along cold fronts.

Current information:

The weather report has shown a cold front above your town. There is a strong wind. Looking out of the window you can see large cumulonimbus clouds. There was a strong red colouration of the sky that morning.

Prediction (consequence of knowing this information):

I predict that…………………………………………………………………….

Prediction Two

Known information:

The more time you spend in a shop, the more you will spend.

The local store manager says that people's shopping habits tend to be set and very difficult to break.

Escalators are at the rear of a shop to make you walk past all the goods on sale.

Shoppers like offers and savings.

My mate says what he wants is always out of stock, and this really annoys him.

Shop staff are trained to ask customers if they need associated items for what they are actually purchasing (for example, to ask if a person needs new socks when they are buying a new pair of shoes).

Some shoppers think that if one item is a bargain in a shop, all the items in that shop must also be bargains.

'Buy one get one free' offers are designed to make consequential thinking about spending money more difficult.

My friend always buys more if they get chatting to the shopkeeper.

Current situation:

A new store has opened in your town. It has advertised heavily in the local papers and you know that the new trainers you wanted are on sale in the store. You use a money saving website to find a discount voucher to take with you. When you arrive at the store, you can see to the back of the store, even though it is packed with lots of goods, and the trainers you want are almost on the last aisle at the back.

Prediction (consequence of knowing this information):

I predict that………………………………………………………………………………..

Prediction Three

Known information:

The media reports that alcohol related violence has increased since the licensing laws were relaxed.

My friends say that alcohol disinhibits him and makes him do silly things.

Alcohol is generally cheaper to buy in bulk.

I tend to get 'mouthy' when I have been drinking.

Alcohol is processed by the liver.

Hangovers are caused by the body recovering from the 'poisoning' effect of alcohol and everyone says they get worse as you get older.

To avoid a hangover, never mix the grape with the grain.

Alcohol is the common name for ethanol compounds.

Current information:

Your friends have invited you round for the evening as it is payday. After a few hours at their flat, you all decide to go into town. Whilst there you go to a club that is offering five drinks for the price of one, and humorously named cocktails. After drinking until the early hours of the morning, you all decide to leave. Outside you run into a large group of equally drunken men. They start to shout and become aggressive even though you and your friends were only trying to walk past. One of the others then shouts that you just made them drop their bottle of drink.

Prediction (consequence of knowing this information)

I predict that……………………………………………………………………….

What are the consequences for you if?

- You got into trouble with the law?

- You ask the facilitator for help with your problems?

Pick a potential solution to a problem you are facing and brainstorm possible the consequences:

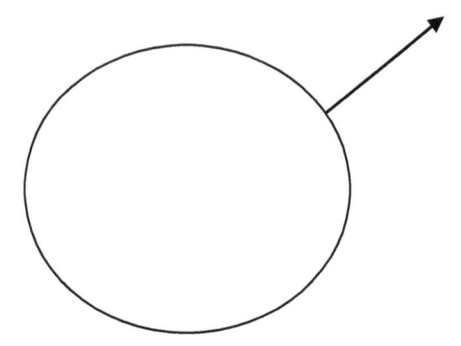

Exercise 8 – Alternative Exercise

This exercise can be presented to the offender as a fun alternative. However, the practitioner must ensure that the end message of consequential thinking is understood and re-enforced at the end of the session.

Step 1: Using 10 sheets of white paper only, write 5 'good things' and 5 'bad things', (one on each sheet of paper) with the client. The good and bad things need to be specific to the client but can be goals, aims, or material objects.

Step 2: Scrunch each piece of paper up into a separate ball (as ball shaped as you can make it) and mix them up so it is no longer possible to tell which 'ball' contains a good item and which contains a bad one.

Step 3: Arrange the balls in a classic 10 pin bowling set up and place a length of string/rope horizontally behind the balls on the floor, as below:

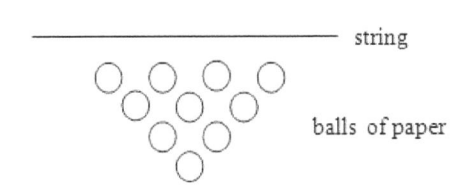

_____ string

○ ○ ○ ○
 ○ ○ ○   balls of paper
  ○ ○
   ○

Step 4: Provide the offender with another scrunched up ball of paper, preferably in another colour to make it identifiable, and facing the apex of the triangle, ask them to 'bowl' one of the balls across the line. They can take as many goes as required. The ball that first crosses the line is the 'outcome' for them.

Step 5: Repeat Step 1 but using coloured paper so that 'good' is one colour and 'bad' another, then repeat steps 2 to 4.

Step 6: Ask the client what they think the point of the exercise was and discuss how it relates to consequential thinking.

Tip: If the client struggles to answer, ask them to consider whether they found it easier to plan, predict and aim for a 'good' ball in the first or second game and how they adjusted their behaviour (aim) accordingly.

Exercise 8 – Out of Session Work

In order to further support the understanding of consequences and consequential thinking, the following out of session work can be used.

Step 1: Ask the offender to plan a moment before the next session when they are able to 'people watch'; explain the steps below to them and ask them to carry these out at an opportune time.

Caution: Ensure that the offender knows what is meant by people watching and that they are able to do this in an inoffensive manner.

Step 2: Picking different people at random, consider what they are doing at a particular moment; for example getting on a bus.

Step 3: Consider the actual behaviour of the person being watched at that time in sequence and the consequences for this. So, for the example above – talking to the driver, asking for a ticket, getting a ticket, sitting down, getting home. Then consider an alternative (fictitious) behaviour in sequence and the consequences for that behaviour. So for the previous example, consider how the person on the bus didn't talk to the driver but shouted and used abusive language, they wouldn't get a ticket, the driver may have called the police/security guards, they would have been evicted from the bus, potentially arrested for a public order offence, and maybe received a fine, and they would have had to walk home.

Step 4: At the next session, describe one or two of their most interesting examples.

Exercise 8 – Review

Name at least one thing that has been learned from this exercise.

Additional Notes:

Exercise 9 - Decision scale: How do I pick?

Category of exercise: Weighing up options

> **Tutor Notes**
>
> It may sound like the easiest part of solving a problem is simply 'picking' one of the options that have been generated. However, for many clients, they may have received the message that their choices tend to be 'wrong', either from negative feedback from those around them or through committing offences. Picking a new option, one that they would not normally do, can be a very scary thing to do first time round.
>
> These 'decision scales' break down the *how* of choosing an option. If this workbook is not being presented as a sequence and depending on the client's confidence in this area, the practitioner may find that exercises 6, 7 and 8 are also helpful.

Step 1: Explain to the client that: "Generally, people do the things they want to - for a particular given reason." In other words, we all expect to get some positive effect from the choices we make, whether this is a realistic expectation or not.

Step 2: Explain to the client that: "If we want to act in a certain way, we do so because we tell ourselves that there is some benefit from doing so." So if we can control this form of "talking to oneself" we can control our behaviours – just as explained in *exercise 1* (if this has been used).

Step 3: Explain to the client that one way to control our thoughts is to come up with *evidence* that the decision we are about to make is either a good or bad idea. One tool we can use to help decide if an option is good or bad is a *decision scale*.

Note: This is actually an exercise formally known as a *cost benefit analysis*. The name has been changed here to simplify the exercise.

Step 4: With the client, decide on either their offence or a problematic situation they are facing, such as 'taking duvet days from work'.

Step 5: Show the client the decision scale and ask the client to consider all the positive elements to the chosen scenario. The facilitator should then list all the positives that the client comes up with. The facilitator should note here that *no answer is wrong*. This is important, as the client's answers are very individualistic to that person.

Note: Both the practitioner and the offender need to be able to accept that there are, and must be, positives to offending/problem behaviours, otherwise we simply wouldn't do it.

Step 6: Ask the client to list all the negatives of the same scenario. Again the facilitator should promote responses by indicating that no answer is wrong. The facilitator should also ask the client to consider areas such as finances, relationships, etc. If the client is really struggling then they can use the fact that they are having to spend time looking at their behaviour as a negative factor.

Step 7: Ask the client to visualise a set of balanced weight scales. Ask the client to draw a horizontal line on the *balanced scales* across the apex of the triangle, to demonstrate the balanced nature of the scales visually on the worksheet. Use the top set of scales on the worksheet labelled 'balanced scales' for this part of the exercise.

Step 8: Ask the client to consider the answers they gave (in steps 5 and 6) as weights to be placed on the scales. Here the facilitator should ask the client to draw the scales as to how they would look if they were able to put their 'weights' on the scales; do the positive factors amount to a heavier or lighter load than the negatives? Ask the client to redraw the horizontal line from the balanced scales onto the *my scales* set of scales, with the correct orientation downwards for either the positive or negative side, depending on their answers.

Tip: It is not about the number of facts on each side of the balance scales. One single fact may 'weigh' more heavily than another. For example the offender may feel that the only negative they were able to identify of 'losing my freedom' is worth more weight than all the positives they identified. This is fine; simply allow the balance line to be drawn to reflect this.

Step 9: The facilitator should then ask the client something to the effect of: "Do the negatives of your behaviour outweigh the positives?" Discuss the client's responses. Also, ask the client to write something they have learned and can take away from the session at the bottom of the worksheet.

Note: If a client feels that the positives of their problem behaviour/offending use outweigh the negatives, this is not necessarily 'end game' for the intervention. What it does show the practitioner is how the offender feels about their behaviour and therefore at what level to start and base the intervention. Roll with the resistance (see section one) and work with the offender over different sessions to challenge their attitude towards this.

Exercise 9 – Worksheet

Is it really worth it chart?

Positives/good things	Negatives/bad things

△ Balanced
  Scales

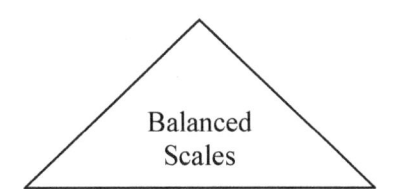

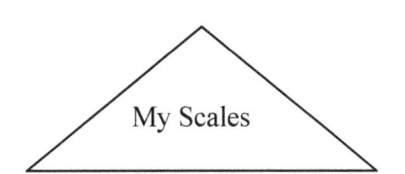

△ My Scales

What do these completed scales mean to you?

Exercise 9a - Alternative Exercise

For the kinaesthetic and visual learners the following exercise is a great alternative, but it does require the facilitator to do a little work beforehand.

Step 1: The facilitator should cut out all the "sometimes" statements in worksheet 9a(i).

Step 2: The facilitator should then shuffle the sometimes statements and read out each statement deciding together with the client if each statement is relevant and where it could go on the scales on worksheet 9a(ii). If a statement is thought to be relevant, place it on top of the line.

Step 3: The tutor should ask the client if they have any additional statements they would like to give about the effect that their problem behaviour sometimes has on them. Write these on the blank statements on worksheet 9a(i). Then, place the answers on the scales.

Step 4: The facilitator should ask the client to count how many negatives statements there are and also how many positive statements there are. Following this, discuss if it is a good decision or not to behave in an offending manner.

Tip: It is not about the number of facts for each side of the balance scales. One single fact may 'weigh' heavier than another. For example the offender may feel that the only negative they were able to identify of 'sometimes I lose my freedom' is worth more weight than all the positives they identified. This is fine; simply reflect this in the final discussion about their behaviour.

Step 5: At the end of the session, the tutor should ask the client to consider what the learning points were of the exercise and then complete the bottom of the worksheet

Exercise 9a(i) Worksheet

The 'behaviour' concerned in the statement is the problem or offending behaviour.

Sometimes my behaviour allows me to get my own way	Sometimes I lose my freedom because of my behaviour	Sometimes my behaviour amuses me	Sometimes I feel that my behaviour is expected of me
Sometimes my behaviour is more trouble than it's worth	Sometimes I am happier when I behave in that manner	Sometimes my behaviour has a bad effect on my relationship	Sometimes my behaviour makes me sad
Sometimes my behaviour causes me to lose things I want/need	Sometimes I can get angry when I am prevented from doing the behaviour I want to	Sometimes I like the effect my behaviour has on people	Sometimes I do not like the effect my behaviour has on people
Sometimes I get fed up with being labelled by other people's view of my behaviour	Sometimes I enjoy my behaviour	Sometimes I gain from my behaviour	Sometimes I lose out from my behaviour
Sometimes ...	Sometimes ...	Sometimes ...	Sometimes ...

Exercise 9a (ii) Worksheet

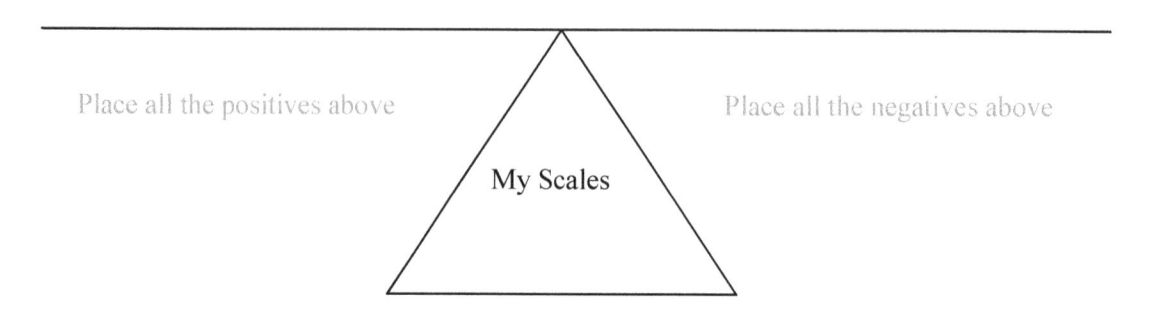

Place all the positives above   Place all the negatives above

My Scales

What can I learn from these completed scales?

Exercise 9 - Out of Session Work

Should the facilitator be of the view that the client would benefit from further exploration of this area, then the facilitator can of course provide out of session work.

The idea of exercise 9 is to enable the client to 'weigh up' each side of an argument in their head and be able to then apply this to varying situations; hopefully and especially the ones that lead them to offend. This skill also requires being able to view situations from another perspective, even if they don't agree with it, in order to generate new ideas. The suggested out of session work is therefore a game of 'devil's advocate'.

Step 1: Run through the exercise steps below before the end of the session to ensure that the client fully understands what they need to do.

Step 2: Explain that a *devil's advocate* is a colloquial term to describe someone who always argues the other side of what someone else is saying, regardless of the situation or their own view.

Step 3: Read through the worksheet together and ask the offender to complete it prior to the next session: completing the empty boxes and adding more arguments to the completed side.

Step 4: Explain that the blank boxes are there to provide space for the offender's own examples, if they find any during the time between sessions.

Exercise 9 – Out of Session Worksheet

Statement	For	Against
Famous people these days aren't talented	Anyone can get '15 minutes' of fame Televised talent shows don't pick 'talent' – they pick 'amusing'.	
Criminal justice sentencing in the UK is too easy on the criminals		The media doesn't always report the full facts. Full assessments are made to make sure sentences are appropriate. People who say this tend not to have experienced the justice system.
America faked the moon landings	The president was running out of time to get a man to the moon as it was an election promise.	It's too much work to think they could have hidden the fact from other space nations.

Exercise 9 – Review

Name at least one thing that has been learned from this exercise.

Additional Notes:

Exercise 10 – Ending and Reviews (the 3R's)

Category of exercise – Weighing up options

Tutor Notes

The cyclical nature of problem solving is such that having generated options, weighed them up, picked one and acted on it – it is still not the end of the tale. The resultant consequences of the 'solution' need to be looked at. Has the problem *actually* been solved? The client needs to be able to differentiate between solutions which are like spitting in to a headwind, or putting up a windbreak.

In the problem solving sequence for this workbook, this step is called 'the three Rs', for no other reason than to make it memorable. The three Rs are – review, resolved and reoccurs.

Review – there is some improvement in the situation, but it's not quite right. This would result in needing to go back to the 'generating options' stage and looking for a new solution to try out, but one that it similar to that originally trialled. It's about being able to find the ideal jigsaw piece for your puzzle, not just a near enough fit.

Resolved – this speaks for itself. The solution gives the desired positive result.

Reoccurs – the problem happens again. Many of the options generated have been tried, or at least brainstormed for likely consequences. The solutions trialled have had *no effect* or even exacerbated the problem, and as such the client needs to go back to the start of the sequence and redo the problem solving, potentially being more detailed about the problem and/or looking for new perspectives on possible solutions.

Tip: depending on the learning style of the client, this exercise can be presented simply as a verbal discussion rather than cutting/folding the paper as described below.

Step 1: For each problem and tried solution scenario, cut out the three boxes below and fold each box in half so that the information on it cannot be seen. Label each piece of paper on the outside either 'review', 'reoccur', or 'resolved'.

Step 2: With the client, explain the 3 Rs as above.

Step 3: Go through the scenarios and ask the client, based on their understanding of Step 2, whether the next stage is to review the solution, consider it resolved, whether the problem has reoccurred?

Step 4: Open the folded piece of paper which corresponds to the client's answer from Step 3. Discuss whether they were correct, or if their answer differs - why it differs. The facilitator can provide more than one opportunity to select an answer.

Note: Although a client may answer differently to the 'correct' answer, it may be that they have a very reasonable explanation for this which nulls the scenario answer. This is fine if they are able to explain and evidence their choice. As always, challenge inappropriate answers.

Step 5: Continue for the other two examples and then ask the client for examples of problems they have experienced where they could fit their solutions into each of the three Rs.

Exercise 10 – Worksheet

Martin was driving on the M1 when he noticed that the steering on his car felt wrong; the car was pulling hard to the left. After running through the problem solving sequence in his head, Martin decided that a good option would be to continue to the next service station, as stopping on the hard shoulder is for emergencies and can in itself be dangerous. Initially the car felt under control but then after about another half a mile, the pulling on the steering wheel increased.

Consider whether the Martin's choice of solution has **resolved** the problem, whether he needs to **review** the problem, or whether the problem has **reoccurred**.

REVIEW	REOCCUR	RESOLVED
The problem was initially under control. However, when it began to worsen, Martin can go back to the 'generating options' stage of problem solving and pick 'stop on the hard shoulder' as the car is now clearly too dangerous to drive at speed.	Martin had not yet exhausted possible or probable solutions from his initial 'generating options' stage and still had some viable solutions to try.	No. The problem has not been resolved. In fact, it has got worse.

Emily came home after a night out with friends and found that she did not have her front door keys on her. She quickly thought through the problem solving sequence and decided on the options of shouting to try and wake her flat mate up, breaking in, and emptying her bag to look for the keys. After shouting, Emily realised her flatmate's car was not on the drive. She was not able to find her keys in her bag and when she thought about whether to try and break in she realised that the burglar alarm was likely to be on and that this would set it off.

Consider whether Emily's choice of solutions has **resolved** the problem, whether she needs to **review** the problem, or whether the problem has **reoccurred**.

REVIEW	REOCCUR	RESOLVED
None of the solutions have come close to solving the problem. It is likely that Emily was not detailed enough in her definition of the problem and did not consider the problem from other perspectives.	Emily has been through all of the viable options she initially generated and none of them have resolved the problem. She needs to go back and start again. What other perspective on her problem can you think of?	No. The problem has not been resolved.

Ian was late for work. He had recently lost his driving licence due to an accrual of points from speeding but had not yet sold his car, which was still sat on his driveway. Ian knows that if he is late to work again, he is likely to lose his employment. Using the problem solving sequence, he considers his options to be: driving the car anyway and hoping he doesn't get caught, getting the bus and being late, or getting a taxi with the money he had hoped to save for going out at the weekend. Ian brainstorms the potential consequences of each option and decides to get a taxi.

Consider whether Ian's choice of solution has **resolved** the problem, whether he needs to **review** the problem, or whether the problem has **reoccurred**.

REVIEW	REOCCUR	RESOLVED
The problem has been resolved in the immediacy. It may be worth Ian reviewing the bigger problem of why he was late for work and solving this to prevent his lateness happening again.	Ian still had two options left before he was out of solutions. His consequential thinking meant that he ruled out breaking the law but he could have been late on the bus and hoped his boss would understand.	Yes. Ian has resolved the problem of being late for work, in this instance. He may benefit from problem solving the bigger problem of why he is late for work to prevent a repeat of this lateness.

Think of problems you have encountered in your life where you **reviewed** the solution options generated, felt that your solutions **resolved** the situation, or where the problem **reoccurred**. Note these below and explain how you think the example fits in to each of the categories:

An example where the problem was resolved:

_____

_____

_____

_____

An example where the problem reoccurred (what did you do about this?):

_____

_____

_____

_____

An example where the situation needed to be reviewed:

_____

_____

_____

_____

Exercise 10 – Alternative Exercise

This exercise has been written with the more kinaesthetic learner in mind. It does require a little preparation from the practitioner.

To recap from above, in the problem solving sequence for this workbook, this step is called 'the three Rs', for no other reason than to make it memorable. The three Rs are – review, resolved and reoccurs.

Review – there is some improvement in the situation, but it's not quite right. This would result in needing to go back to the 'generating options' stage and looking for a new solution to try out, but one that it similar to that originally trialled. It's about being able to find the ideal jigsaw piece for your puzzle, not just a near enough fit.

Resolved – this speaks for itself. The solution gives the desired positive result.

Reoccurs – the problem happens again. Many of the options generated have been tried, or at least brainstormed for likely consequences. The solutions trialled have had *no effect* or even exacerbated the problem, and as such the client needs to go back to the start of the sequence and redo the problem solving, potentially being more detailed about the problem and/or looking for new perspectives on possible solutions.

Step 1: Cut out and form the die on worksheet 10a(i). Find two coins to use as counters.

Step 2: Explain the concept of the three Rs to the client, as described above, and check their understanding.

Step 3: Starting with the counters at the beginning of the board on Worksheet 10a(ii), the client should roll the die. If the result from the die makes sense with the next action that the person in the scenario should take, and the client can provide an example of this (in keeping with the scenario), then the client can move their counter forwards.

For example, the first scenario would really require the person concerned to *review* their solution and a way they could do this. If the roll of the die produces an answer which does not fit, then the practitioner can have a go.

Step 4: The first person to reach the end of the board wins. The practitioner must make sure at the end of the 'game' that the client understands the concept of the three Rs.

Exercise 10a Worksheet(i)

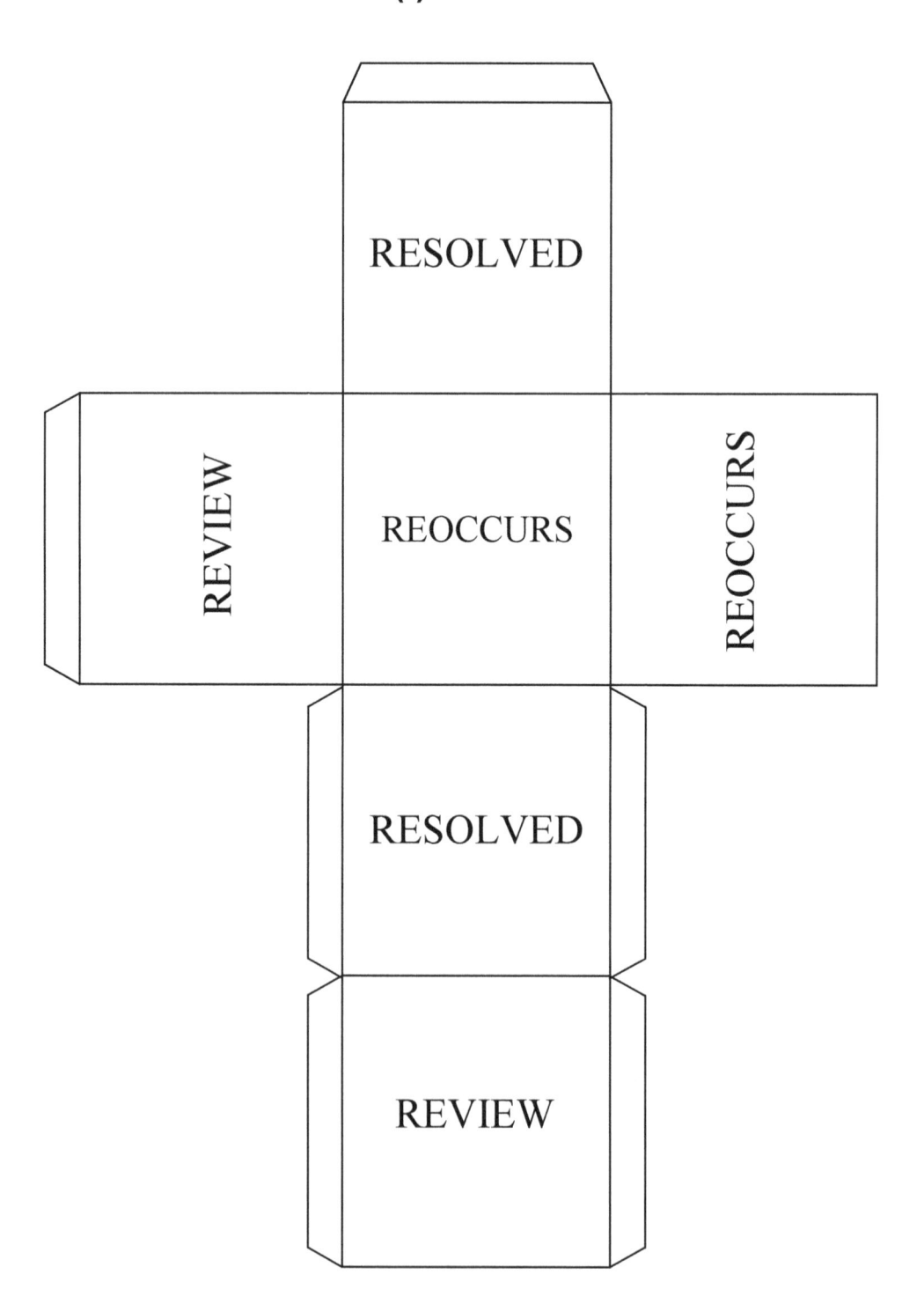

RESOLVED

REVIEW   REOCCURS   REOCCURS

RESOLVED

REVIEW

Exercise 10a – Worksheet (ii)

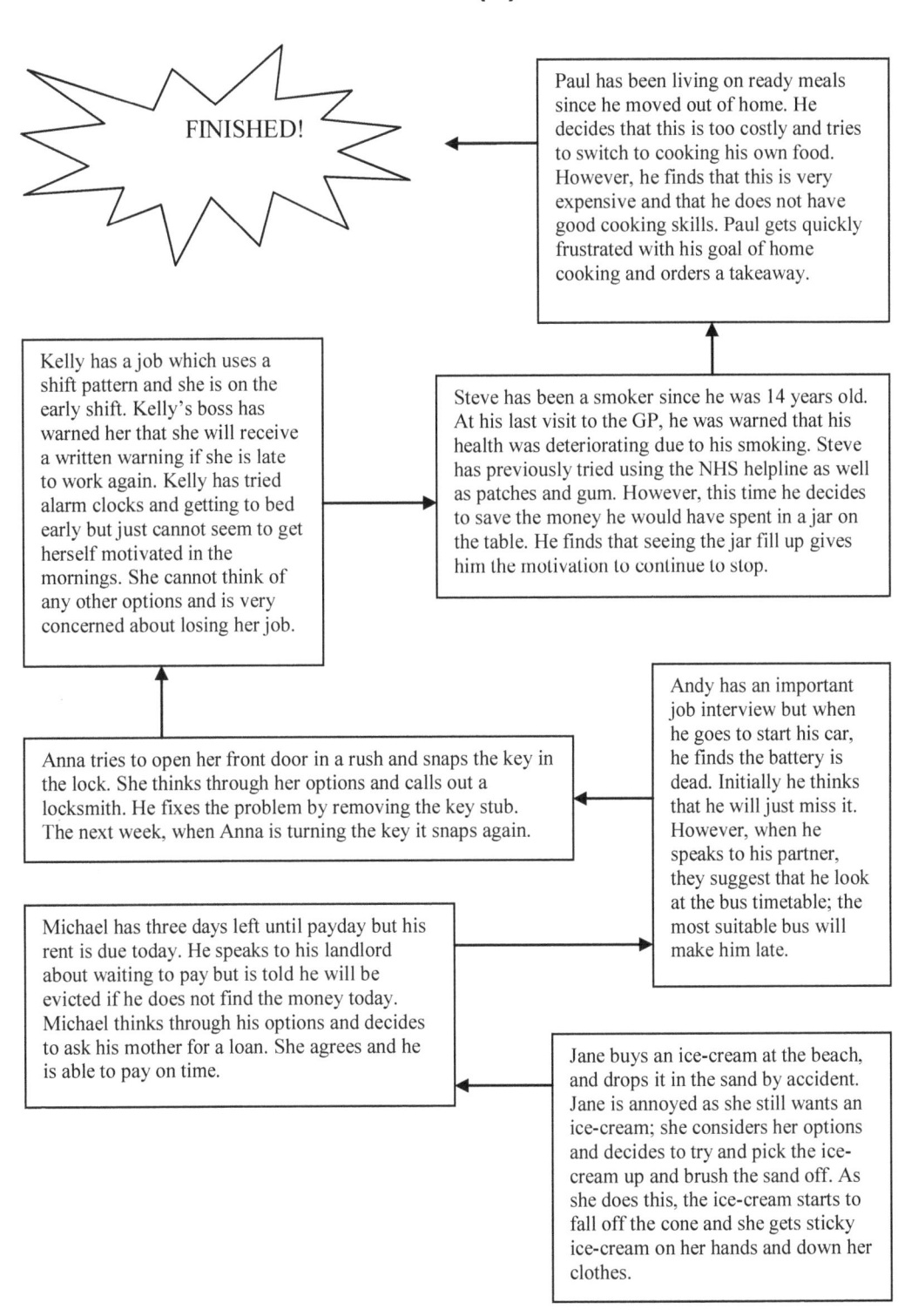

FINISHED!

Paul has been living on ready meals since he moved out of home. He decides that this is too costly and tries to switch to cooking his own food. However, he finds that this is very expensive and that he does not have good cooking skills. Paul gets quickly frustrated with his goal of home cooking and orders a takeaway.

Kelly has a job which uses a shift pattern and she is on the early shift. Kelly's boss has warned her that she will receive a written warning if she is late to work again. Kelly has tried alarm clocks and getting to bed early but just cannot seem to get herself motivated in the mornings. She cannot think of any other options and is very concerned about losing her job.

Steve has been a smoker since he was 14 years old. At his last visit to the GP, he was warned that his health was deteriorating due to his smoking. Steve has previously tried using the NHS helpline as well as patches and gum. However, this time he decides to save the money he would have spent in a jar on the table. He finds that seeing the jar fill up gives him the motivation to continue to stop.

Anna tries to open her front door in a rush and snaps the key in the lock. She thinks through her options and calls out a locksmith. He fixes the problem by removing the key stub. The next week, when Anna is turning the key it snaps again.

Andy has an important job interview but when he goes to start his car, he finds the battery is dead. Initially he thinks that he will just miss it. However, when he speaks to his partner, they suggest that he look at the bus timetable; the most suitable bus will make him late.

Michael has three days left until payday but his rent is due today. He speaks to his landlord about waiting to pay but is told he will be evicted if he does not find the money today. Michael thinks through his options and decides to ask his mother for a loan. She agrees and he is able to pay on time.

Jane buys an ice-cream at the beach, and drops it in the sand by accident. Jane is annoyed as she still wants an ice-cream; she considers her options and decides to try and pick the ice-cream up and brush the sand off. As she does this, the ice-cream starts to fall off the cone and she gets sticky ice-cream on her hands and down her clothes.

Exercise 10 – Out of Session Work

Exercise 10 is about reviewing and revising our decisions rather than plunging blindly ahead. If more support is required to reinforce this idea with the client, ask them to consider (between sessions) behaviours that they routinely do without thinking, such as smoking or watching TV in the evenings. Ask them to consider whether this behaviour is working for them (a decision scale) and what other options they may have. The client needs to feedback their findings at the next session.

Exercise 10 – Review

Name at least one thing that has been learned from this exercise.

Additional Notes:

Exercise 11 – Problem Solving Sequence Reviewed

Category of exercise: General thinking skills

Tutor Notes

Here the facilitator should cut out the problem solving steps in worksheet 11(a) and work with the client to put them in the correct order as a form of review as to whether the client is able to recall the sequence. Ask the client to provide an example problem and work it through the sequence. This can either be a problem they have already solved or one that requires solving.

Following this, as a conclusion to the preceding exercises (if the workbook has been used in sequence), use worksheet 11(b) and ask the client to consider and write down (with the facilitator helping to jog their memory) all the learning points from previous sessions and the goals they have achieved.

Tip: This is a great way to measure outcomes from this intervention.

Exercise 11 – Worksheet 11(a)

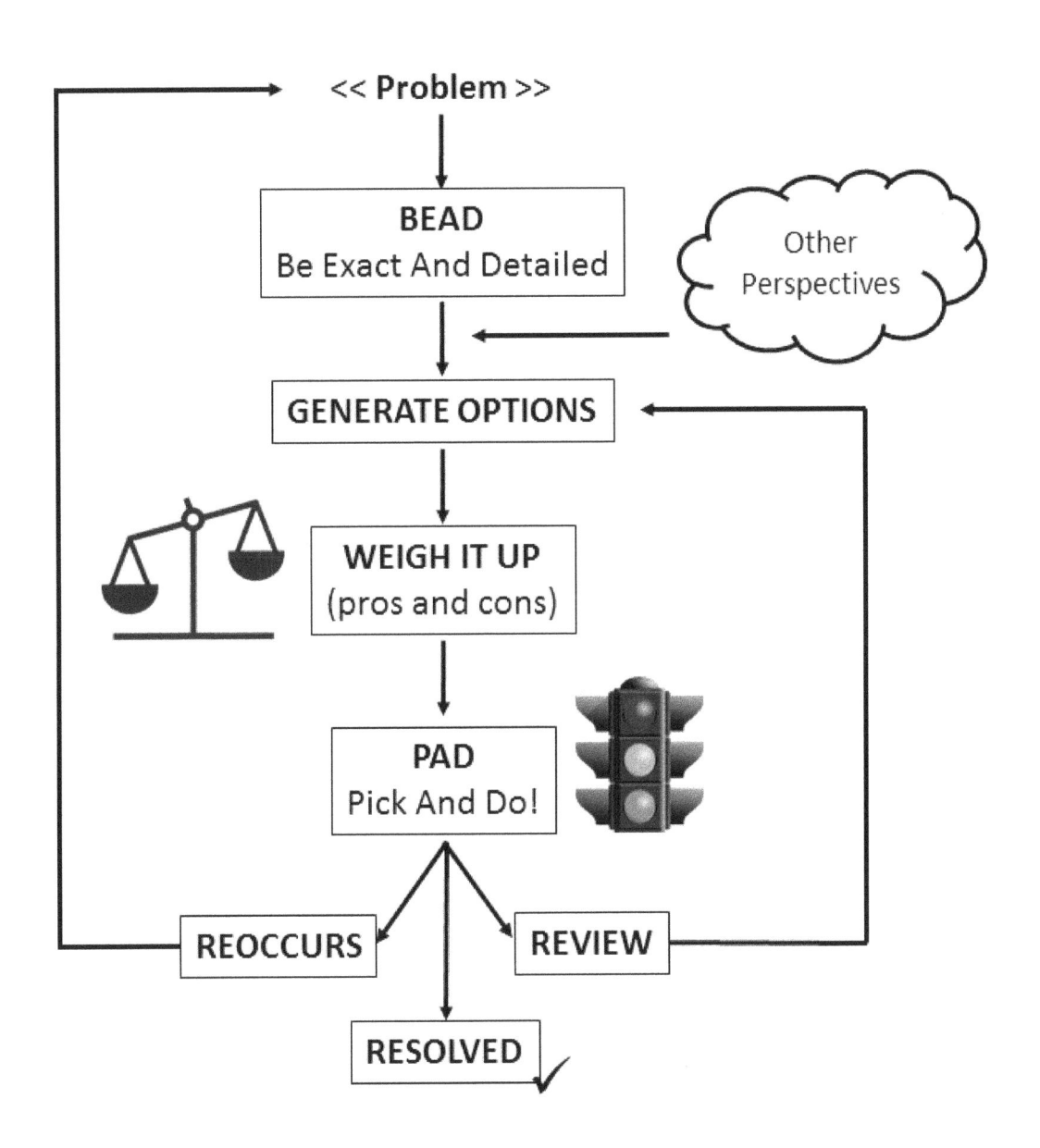

```
            << Problem >>
                 │
                 ▼
        ┌─────────────────┐
        │      BEAD       │         ╭─────────────╮
        │ Be Exact And    │         │    Other    │
        │    Detailed     │         │ Perspectives │
        └─────────────────┘         ╰─────────────╯
                 │       ◄─────────────┘
                 ▼
        ┌─────────────────┐  ◄──────────────┐
        │ GENERATE OPTIONS│                 │
        └─────────────────┘                 │
                 │                          │
                 ▼                          │
        ┌─────────────────┐                 │
        │   WEIGH IT UP   │                 │
        │ (pros and cons) │                 │
        └─────────────────┘                 │
                 │                          │
                 ▼                          │
        ┌─────────────────┐                 │
        │      PAD        │                 │
        │   Pick And Do!  │                 │
        └─────────────────┘                 │
            ↙     ↓     ↘                   │
    ┌──────────┐  │  ┌────────┐             │
    │ REOCCURS │  │  │ REVIEW │ ────────────┘
    └──────────┘  │  └────────┘
                  ▼
            ┌──────────┐
            │ RESOLVED │ ✓
            └──────────┘
```

(REOCCURS loops back to Problem)

Exercise 11 – Review – Worksheet 11(b)

Write down what you have learned from the exercises in this workbook.

1.

2.

3.

4.

5.

6.

7.

8.

9.

10.

11.

12.

Now review the goals set in exercise 3 and where appropriate set new ones:

Goal 1 was:

| |
| |

I feel I have/have not (delete as applicable) achieved this because:

| |
| |

Moving forwards, my new goal here is to:

| |
| |

Goal 2 was:

I feel I have/have not (delete as applicable) achieved this because:

Moving forwards, my new goal here is to:

Goal 3 was:

[ ]

I feel I have/have not (delete as applicable) achieved this because:

[ ]

Moving forwards, my new goal here is to:

[ ]

Exercise 12 – Reflections

Category of exercise: General thinking skills

Tutor Notes

This exercise has been purposely put after the review of the workbook. Reflecting is an important skill which enables us to constantly look over our behaviour, lives and choices and in some instances, make changes *before* significant problems erupt.

Reflecting on ourselves is just like looking in a mirror and then commentating on the reflection using all the skills involved in the problem solving sequence – defining problems, perspective taking, generating options, consequential thinking and weighing up options.

Step 1: Using the worksheet, ask the offender to look into the 'mirror' and imagine they can see their reflection.

Step 2: Write around the edge of the mirror what they can 'see'. This needs to include both physical attributes and non-visible ones, such as 'friendly' or 'easily led'.

Step 3: Go through the points the offender has identified and briefly discuss whether any of these need to be reviewed for their 'value'. Ask the offender "Does [insert observation] make a positive contribution to your life?" If they answer 'no' then use the problem solving sequence to look at how this identified problem can be addressed.

Step 4: Look in the mirror *with* the offender and add any observations that you feel the offender has missed. Discuss these as per Step 3.

Caution: This is not an opportunity for the facilitator to judge the offender. Both positive and negative observations need to be made. If a negative one is made, it needs to be carefully presented and backed up with actual evidence, not just the facilitator's opinion. For example, the facilitator may say "I can also see someone who is easily led by some of their peers. Do you remember when you told me about the time that…"

Please note, there is no alternative exercise or out of session work here. This exercise is a significant piece of work if done properly and can be easily adapted to all learning styles and literacy levels.

Exercise 12 – Worksheet

Look in to the mirror – what do you see…?

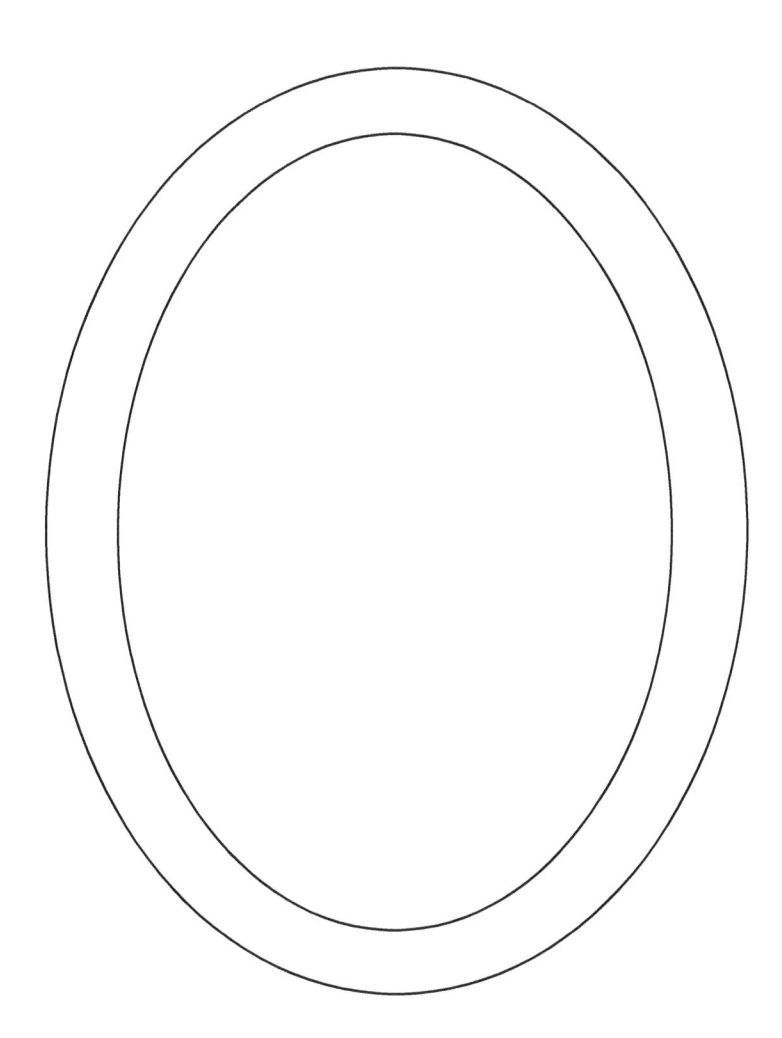

Lightning Source UK Ltd.
Milton Keynes UK
UKHW032107271220
375841UK00010B/838